Manila
Envelopes

MANILA ENVELOPES

Oregon Volunteer Lt. George F. Telfer's

Spanish-American War Letters

edited
by
SARA BUNNETT

OREGON HISTORICAL SOCIETY
PRESS

Frontis: Lt. George F. Telfer. (Author's collection)

Production of this publication was generously supported in part by contributions from the following persons:
Joseph F. and Sara A. Bunnett, Arnold Challman and family, Cary Heath, Charles R. Heath, Abby Telfer, and Mary A. and William H. Telfer.

Produced and designed by The Oregon Historical Society Press.

Maps by John Tomlinson and Johanna Neshyba.

Library of Congress Cataloging-in-Publication Data

Telfer, George F. (George Fillmore), 1855–1930.
    Manila envelopes.

    Bibliography: p.
    Includes index.
    1. Telfer, George F. (George Fillmore), 1855–1930—Correspondence.   2. United States—History—War of 1898—Personal narratives.   3. Oregon. National Guard—Biography.   4. Soldiers—Oregon—Correspondence.
I. Bunnett, Sara.   II. Title.
E729.T45 1986   973.8'98   [B]   86–5484
ISBN 0-87595-129-5 (pbk.)

FOR ALL THE

LETTER WRITERS
&
LETTER SAVERS

Contents

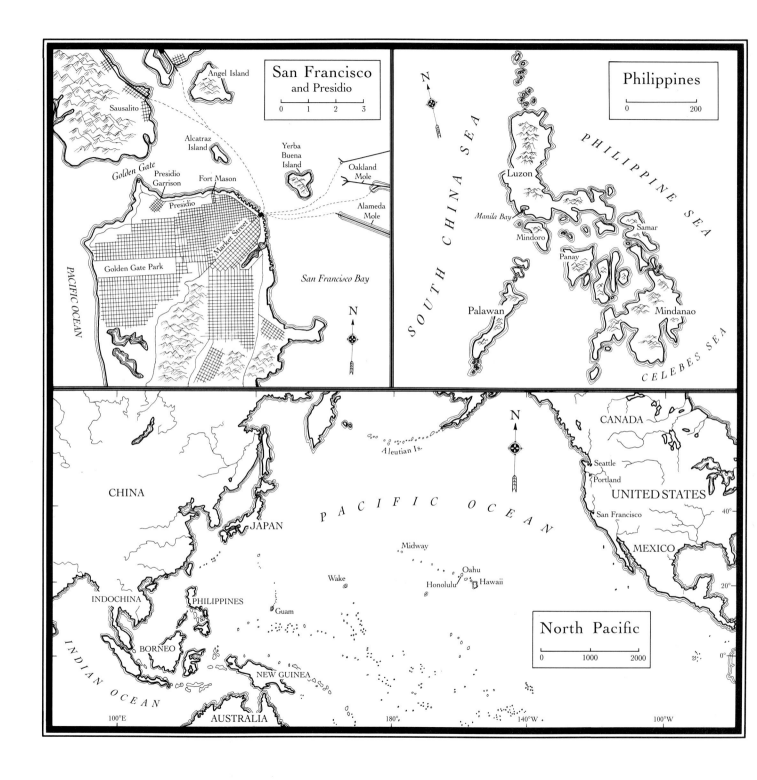

San Francisco
and Presidio

0   1   2   3

Angel Island

Sausalito

Alcatraz
Island

Golden Gate

Presidio
Garrison

Presidio

Fort Mason

Yerba
Buena
Island

Oakland
Mole

Alameda
Mole

Market Street

Golden Gate Park

PACIFIC
OCEAN

San Francisco Bay

N

Philippines

0   200

N

SOUTH CHINA SEA

PHILIPPINE SEA

Luzon

Manila Bay

Mindoro

Panay

Samar

Palawan

Mindanao

CELEBES SEA

CANADA

Aleutian Is.

CHINA

JAPAN

PACIFIC OCEAN

Seattle
Portland

UNITED STATES

San Francisco

40°

MEXICO

Midway

Oahu

Honolulu   Hawaii

20°

Wake

INDOCHINA

PHILIPPINES

Guam

North Pacific

0   1000   2000

BORNEO

NEW GUINEA

INDIAN OCEAN

100°E

AUSTRALIA

180°

140°W

100°W

0°

Introduction

For much of America, the 1890s ushered in a period of tremendous social and economic prosperity. Revitalized ideals of freedom and patriotic strength, established during the post-Civil War Reconstruction, had thirty years to develop, creating a nation with a backbone of dauntless, almost anxious pride.

For the country's near island neighbor to the south, however, this national "freedom" was still an aspiration which meant little less than insurrection. Cuba, long held as a Spanish colony, had already been witness to dire political unrest. Cuban patriots had spent a decade struggling for independence from Spain (Ten Years War of 1868–78), and accomplished little political change as a result.

Continued revolt against Spanish imperial rule began to draw upon the sympathies of the United States press. Americans could not help but be aware of developments in such a near neighbor; and as Spanish treatment of Cuban rebels appeared to become increasingly inhumane, the U.S. "yellow press" took ample advantage of an opportunity to turn American sentiment against Spain. In addition to these unsettling circumstances, Spanish guerrilla warfare brought about heavy losses in American investments. Thus, a mounting cycle of journalistic and military propaganda set American public opinion in a retaliatory fervor. Finally, when the USS *Maine* mysteriously exploded in Havana's harbor on 15 February 1898, President McKinley had little option but to ask Congress for a declaration of war.

In addition to these disturbances in Cuba, other U.S. officials, primarily Secretary of the Navy Theodore Roosevelt, were secretly preparing to seize Spain's western Pacific possessions, the Philippines. Immediately after war was declared Secretary Roosevelt took it upon himself to send orders to George Dewey, commodore in charge of the American Asiatic Squadron in the Pacific, to leave the China coast and head toward Manila. The squadron arrived in Manila Bay on 1 May 1898 and proceeded to carry out orders by destroying the once powerful Spanish fleet. As a consequence, Dewey was promoted directly to admiral and the United States was given its first hero of the war.

While this unexpected act of aggression was viewed by the United States as an overwhelming victory, it did not constitute the taking of Manila. Dewey's naval forces had essentially taken the first steps toward invading Spanish-occupied Manila, yet had insufficient on-board American troops to take possession of the city. The American fleet was thus forced to wait off the coast of the Philippines for more than three months until 13 August 1898, when expeditionary forces arrived to relieve them and take the city.

The Spanish-American War established a new world role for the United States. Blithely and hubristically, America entered into a war it was not prepared to fight. In 1898 there were fewer than thirty thousand men in the regular army. Up until the day the war began, the army seemed to have considered no contingencies beyond Indian fighting. It had no high command, no war plans, no experience in transporting large-unit operations overseas, and no formal liaison with the navy. Their "unpreparedness," however, was certainly no reflection of their enthusiasm. Lack of manpower in the regular army was compensated for by an abundance of volunteers in nearly forty-five National Guard "state armies."

Prior to 1898, these National Guard units had served primarily social and political duties rather than military obligations.[1] As self-sufficient, state-run organizations, they not only elected their own officers, but also voted whether or not to go to war. Because the units were initially forbidden to fight overseas, military officials considered dissolving them and enlisting members individually in the U.S. Army.

The guardsmen, however, valued their local identity and were adamantly set against losing it. Mutual appeasement came when Congress decided to create an independent federal force. Thus, a National Guard unit could be called up as a body, should its state governor approve. Further, the regimental officers were appointed by the president on the recommendation of each state's governor. The end result allowed each militia to retain its own identity and its own commanders.

Retaining their own identity, unfortunately, brought with it some drawbacks. The National Guard had no national uniformity of organization, equipment, or expertise. Guardsmen's firearms differed from those of the regular army, and some even required ammunition no longer manufactured in this country. However, because of the existence of these locally sponsored military units, the national budget for defense could be kept to a minimum. The army's share of the War Department budget was only what was required to maintain coastal defenses and units to fight Indian wars.

A week before war was declared, a statement had been issued by the War Department that only the National Guard would be allowed to volunteer on the first call for troops. Oregon was asked to provide one infantry regiment. Since the Oregon National Guard (ONG) was a single brigade composed of two regiments, not all the men could go. After consolidating and reorganizing the companies, only Company H of the First Regiment, ONG, was enlisted intact. The eleven remaining companies of the new regiment, to be called the Second Oregon Volunteers, were formed by consolidations.[2] Company L, commanded by Capt. Harry Wells and 1st Lt. George F. Telfer, was made up of men from Company K, First Regiment, and Company G, Third Battalion.

The rendezvous point for the entire Oregon guard was Portland, where the screening and selection of volunteers took place. The Irvington Race Track became Camp McKinley, and by 3 May 1898, the whole brigade of the ONG was encamped there. Lieutenant Colonel C.E. Gantenbein was the commanding officer of Camp McKinley. Those volunteering to join the ONG were not only required to pass a physical examination, but an inspection of character and professional ability. So many failed the physical that Gov. William P. Lord wired Washington for permission to relax the rules for volunteers.[3] With this done, the regiment was finally formed, and the *Oregonian* of 8 May 1898 announced a dress parade at Camp McKinley, for which admission of a dime was charged.

On the eleventh of May the Second Oregon Volunteers began moving south to San Francisco via the Southern Pacific Railroad. By the sixteenth of May companies L and M, the last to be mustered in, had departed, and Camp McKinley was once again a meadow at the race track in Irvington Park.

The original campaign for the Philippines provided for the movement of the First California Volunteer Infantry and a battalion of the 14th U.S. Infantry to Manila by way of a transport, loading at San Francisco with naval stores for Adm. George Dewey.[4] It was later decided that the Second Oregon Volunteers would be added to this expedition, provid-

ing ships could be found. Two small transports were located: the SS *Australia*, owned by Oceanic Steamships Company, which was chartered for $20,000 per month; and the *City of Sydney*, which was chartered for $1,000 per day.

Two days before sailing, Lt. Ralph Platt, commissary for the regiment, received six months' regular army rations. He was ordered to store five months' rations in the hold of the *Australia* and retain the rest for use on the voyage. At the same time he was ordered to inspect the ship's commissary facilities. He reported that the six-foot square galley, designed to prepare food for three hundred, was totally inadequate for one thousand men, and recommended the purchase of new equipment. However, the representatives of the ship's owners objected, claiming Platt was a "landlubber who didn't understand cooking on a steamship."[5] Platt's request was denied, but the voyage proved him correct in his estimations. The refrigerators were designed to keep beer cold between San Francisco and Honolulu, and were incapable of properly storing the fresh meat ration. As a result, fifteen hundred pounds of meat had to be destroyed during the voyage. It was necessary to cook round the clock in order to provide two meals a day. Without proper equipment, this task was like "trying to roast a quarter of beef in a frying pan," according to Lieutenant Platt.

Complaints about food diminished once the troops were in camp near Manila. Lieutenant Platt attributed this to its being properly cooked, for a change, but it could also be that there were now other things about which to complain. Beyond the lack of modern

Muster in "Camp Portland," 1898. Portland was the rendezvous for selection of the state National Guard companies that formed the Second Oregon Volunteers. (OHS neg. 77442)

rifles and ammunition, the most glaring omissions were in the medical department. The skill of the physicians and surgeons was not at question, but rather the shortage of supplies and nurses. Lieutenant Platt reported that, though they were going to a malaria region, the six-month ration of quinine (used for the treatment of malaria) allowed only four ounces for every one thousand men.[6] Major Herbert W. Card- well, chief surgeon, United States Volunteers (USV) wrote to Gen. Charles F. Beebe in Portland on 25 November 1898, that five months after the first troops landed in the Philippines, medical supplies were ample, but the need for nurses was severe.[7] By nurses, he meant male nurses. Clara Barton notwithstanding, the use of women to nurse men was generally still frowned upon by those in command. The

Second Oregon Volunteers parading in Grants Pass, May 1898. Their destination is
San Francisco and then on to the Philippines. (OHS neg. 77362)

women nurses sent from Oregon did not join the army hospital staff, but set up a separate convalescent hospital just for the Oregon regiment.

While the Oregon National Guard volunteers were in the process of preparing themselves for the rigors of military service, the women of Portland organized themselves to assist the ONG regiment. The state government made no provisions for feeding the men who were coming to Portland for the screening; since there was no Red Cross Society in the city at that time, the women rose to the occasion and made this their first project.

According to the *Oregonian* of 27 April 1898, one hundred women assembled at the Armory to hear Col. O. Summers bring their meeting to order, stating: "the purpose of the moving spirits was to perfect an organization similar to those existing among the women during the civil war under various names. Their first work would be making the stay of the soldiers in Portland, prior to going [to the] East, as pleasant as the nature of Camp life would permit, and cheering them on to their duty. Following that, the requirements of the association would be largely dependent on the issues of war."[8]

Thus was born the Oregon Emergency Corps (OEC), with an executive committee of twelve. Each of these twelve acted as chairwoman of a subcommittee responsible for assisting a single company. Mrs. George F. Telfer was a member of this executive committee. She had five assistants — Mrs. Gen. C.F. Beebe, Mrs. Col. B.B. Tuttle, Mrs. Collins, Mrs. Hiram Mitchell, and Mrs. Lawrence H. Knapp. When the Oregon regiment left Portland, each company's captain was given $100 by the OEC to be used "to relieve the wants of the sick and needy."[9]

With the troops assembled, mustered, and organized, the first fleet of transports was dispatched from the Presidio at San Francisco and set out across the Pacific for the Philippines.

It is here that Lieutenant George F. Telfer begins his correspondence, continuing through his tedious, overcrowded voyage on the *Australia*, to the warm reception in Honolulu, as a witness to the "capture" of Guam from the Spanish, and finally to the arrival in Cavite and capture of Manila. The letters span a thirteen month period (from May 1898 to July 1899), and allow us special insight into the daily drama of a soldier's experience. He brings colonial Manila to life, recounting not only his military duties and procedures, but his impressions of nineteenth-century Filipino culture; the landscape, religion, food, dress, pricing of goods, means of transportation, roles of husbands and wives, and the interesting integration of Spanish traditions and customs.

These letters, published for the first time in this volume, reveal the keenly human side of Lt. George F. Telfer as he sensitively attends to each of his responsibilities as officer, father, and husband. He shares his military life openly with his family, including the often wearisome, sometimes unpredictable, and even frightening contention with war and political unrest in a foreign land.

Biographical Sketch

George Fillmore Telfer was born 12 March 1855 in Buffalo, New York. He was the only child of William G. and Emeline L. (Pratt) Telfer. His boyhood was spent in Milwaukee, Wisconsin. After graduating from Ripon College in Wisconsin, he moved to Minneapolis, where he was city passenger agent for the Minneapolis and St. Louis Railroad.

He married on 26 May 1880 in Waupaca, Wisconsin, Lottie Rebecca Glaze, only child of Anthony Thompson Glaze, founder and for many years editor of the *Ripon Commonwealth*. During their Portland years, Lottie was organist and choir director at St. David's Episcopal Church.

In 1886, when George moved his family from Minnesota to Portland, he took a job as bookkeeper for Lewes and Dryden Printing Company. He was the firm's assistant manager when, in about 1893, the family moved to Albany, where he managed a farm implement store. However, by 1898 and the outbreak of the Spanish-American War, he was again living in Portland, and was a traveling agent for the Acme Harvester Company.

From 1881 to 1886, George and Lottie had three children: Grace, born in November 1881, Willis in December 1884, and Hazel in August 1886.

After his service in the war, he became credit manager for Wadhams and Kerr (wholesale grocers) until 1902, when he moved his family to Seattle. In 1909 he became assistant secretary of the Seattle Merchants Association, from which, under his guidance, evolved the first Retail Credit Bureau. He was a decidedly ambitious man, but substantial financial success eluded him.

George F. Telfer died on 30 October 1930, at the age of 75, in the Washington Veterans Home in Bremerton, where he had resided for three years.

Telfer joined the Minnesota National Guard on 21 March 1883, and was twice called to active service during Indian outbreaks.[10] In 1886 he resigned from the guard because of his move to Portland. About a year later, he joined Oregon's National Guard, where he saw active service during various anti-Chinese riots.[11] Within twelve years, he advanced from commissary sergeant, First Regiment

George F. Telfer and co-workers pictured in Lewes and Dryden Printing Company offices Portland, ca. 1890. (Author's collection)

ONG (25 October 1887) to inspector-general (27 February 1895) on the staff of the commander-in-chief of the ONG (the governor), with the rank of colonel. He resigned this position in order to enroll in the Oregon Infantry Volunteers.

Local pride about Lieutenant Telfer was intense. When he was appointed judge advocate in Manila, the *Milwaukee Sentinel* in Wisconsin did a feature story on his life, with a handsome sketch of the officer who had spent his boyhood in Milwaukee. Familial honor for the soldiers abroad was so marked, in fact, that relatives often shared their letters with local newspapers. Unfortunately this practice created many a tempest, as misconstructions about life in the Philippines brought about charges and counter-charges, always delayed by the six weeks required for travel between Manila and the United States.

Lieutenant Telfer's participation in the war brought about a particularly strenuous time for his family. His wife and three children were required to move in with his widowed mother in order to survive. The four of them probably lived on less than $100 per month (including what Lottie received from working as an organist for St. David's).

The following letters reveal much of Telfer's character and values, as well as the values of society at that time. Reading the newspapers of the day we see that he fit comfortably into the period. Some of his comments in these letters are a bit embarrassing to us today, but they reflect commonly held attitudes and the language of those times.

Journalistic style in 1898 demanded leisure for reading. Sentences were long, involved, and replete with adjectives. Vessels were "stately," regiments "gallant," soldiers "brave," and men "noble!" A front-page story in the *San Francisco Call* of 16 May 1898, reporting the departure of the first expedition to the Philippines, states: "No procession more stately ever plowed the Western seas than that which passed into history when our boys began their long journey." Another example, taken from a post-war publication by the *Oregonian*, entitled *On to Manila*, recounts the voyage this way: "With . . . dangers staring them in the face and the prospect of being cooped up for weeks within the narrow limits of a crowded transport, the brave defenders of the Stars and Stripes cheered at the prospect of doing their share in avenging the *Maine* and prepared to embark upon the greatest journey of invasion since the world began."

George Telfer's daughter, Grace, was custodian of most of these letters during her lifetime. Her granddaughter, Marilyn Coleman Anderson of Minneapolis, donated them to the Oregon Historical Society and has graciously given permission for their publication. The letters to his son, Willis became the property of his daughter, the transcriber and annotater of this volume, and have also been given to the Oregon Historical Society.

Editorial Principles

George F. Telfer's Spanish-American War Letters are here published to illustrate one man's first-hand observations of the American occupation of Manila between 1898 and 1899. The letters were not, of course, written with the intention of publication, and therefore have required some alterations.

Much of Telfer's punctuation and spelling have been regularized for the sake of consistency (for example, dashes have been deleted when directly preceding commas and periods). His references to ships and newspaper names have been italicized to conform with modern usage. Since Telfer was forced to abbreviate many words in order to save letter space (and postage), most of the uncommon abbreviations have been spelled out, along with dates, locations, et cetera. Other, more recognizable abbreviations have been retained and/or regularized.

Spelling has been corrected whenever an inconsistency detracts from the overall comprehension of a sentence. Telfer spelled many place names inconsistently (for example, Honolula, Manilla, et cetera), and these have been corrected. Those errors not directly affecting the meaning have been retained in order to preserve Telfer's original flavor and style.

Manila
Envelopes

Presidio Cal May 20 1898

Dear Family

This is the first moment I have had to write since arrival.

The train trip was uneventful. The men were crowded into emigrant cars The officers had Pullman. We received as much again stuff as could be eaten.

I was Quartermaster of our section. All I had to do was wire ahead for coffee & see to its distribution.

We had a long march from the wharf to camp. And it was after 8 PM before I was located in a tent (Wednesday) Yesterday morning I went on guard & have just been relieved — We were fed by the ladies of the Red Cross Society

when we got off the train and people came out daily with fruit & provisions. Comments on line of march here were very complimentary. And the newspapers say we are the first soldiers to arrive. The "14th" (Vancouver) is camped next to us. They decline to recognize the California Regiment which is on the other side of them. But treat us with all consideration. The California regiment is a mob — very poorly uniformed.

We are in quarantine on account of measels This has some advantage as it keeps the crowds away.

The men have nothing but bacon — hard tack — coffee — & potatoes. — No fresh meat The officers are eating when they get the chance. No

Reproduction of Letter 1. (OHS collections)

Letters

« 1 »

Presidio, Cal.
May 20, 1898

Dear Family,

This is the first moment I have had to write since arrival.

The train trip was uneventful. The men were crowded into emigrant cars. The officers had Pullman. We received as much again stuff as could be eaten.

I was Quartermaster of our section. All I had to do was wire ahead for coffee and see to its distribution.

We had a long march from the wharf to camp. And it was after 8 P.M. before I was located in a tent. (Wednesday) Yesterday morning I went on guard — and have just been relieved. We were fed by the ladies of the Red Cross Society when we got off the train. And people come out daily with fruit and provisions. Comments on line of march here were very complimentary. And the newspapers say we are the first *soldiers* to arrive. The 14th (Vancouver) [U.S. Infantry] is camped next to us. They decline to recognize the California Regiment which is on the other side to them. But treat us with all consideration. The California regiment is a mob — *very* poorly uniformed.

We are in quarantine on account of measels.[12] This has some advantage as it keeps the crowds away.

The men have nothing but bacon — hard tack — coffee — and potatoes. No fresh meat. The officers are eating when they get the chance. No mess arrangements have been made for officers. The men eat on the ground in their own tents or open air. No mess tents. The wind blows constantly and *nothing* is comfortable.

I met Will Darling on the ferry.[13]

Mr. Reed called yesterday and invited me to dinner tonight. I have not been down town yet.

We draw canvas uniforms tomorrow. I think Gen'l Merriam intends sending us with the first party — if we can be gotten in shape — as he is hurrying our equipment ahead of the others.[14]

View of Camp McKinley from judge's stand,
relief guard at right. (OHS neg. 77497)

Will write more description later — when I feel
better. Am going down town this afternoon.

Affectionately,
George

Address:
    Co. "L" 2nd Regt. OR. Vol.
    Presidio
    San Francisco, Cal.

« 2 »

Presidio, Cal.
May 21, 1898

Dear Lottie,

We have received orders to embark Monday morning. Our battalion will likely be on the *Peking* and the
first to land at Manila. The 14th and ours have been
selected out of the lot. I presume some eastern troops
will also go. Of course our men are wild with joy.
They and the 14th stood at the dividing line and
cheered each other for about two hours last night.

I am writing this before breakfast — as I am not
likely to have any more time. The *Oregonian* correspondent will likely keep you well informed as to our
movements. There will be no time to write me. I
understand we are to be paid on board ship. In this
case I will send you money from Honolulu — where
we lay for a day or so.

I have not spent money so far as I have had no
chance. Will draw from emergency fund today for
revolver, etc.

Was at Reed's to dinner last night and got filled up.
Mrs. Raleigh and her daughters called on me yesterday.[15] They all sent lots of love to you, mother and
the children. They are all lovely. Harry is an artist
and has earned a scholarship and is supporting himself. He is coming out today. I am invited there for
dinner Sunday. There was a Mrs. Winch with them —
a sister in law of the one you know. She visits the
Buchtells shortly and has promised to hunt you up
and report on my condition.[16]

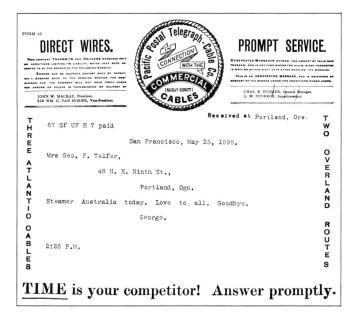

DIRECT WIRES. **PROMPT SERVICE.**

Pacific Postal Telegraph-Cable Co.
IN CONNECTION WITH THE COMMERCIAL CABLES

JOHN W. MACKAY, President.
SIR WM. C. VAN HORNE, Vice-President.

CHAS. R. HOSMER, General Manager.
L. W. STORROR, Superintendent.

Received at Portland, Ore.

T H R E E   A T L A N T I C   C A B L E S

67 Sf UF E 7 paid

San Francisco, May 25, 1898.

Mrs Geo. F. Telfer,

48 N. E. Ninth St.,

Portland, Ogn.

Steamer Australia today. Love to all. Goodbye.

George.

2:26 P.M.

T W O   O V E R L A N D   R O U T E S

TIME is your competitor! Answer promptly.

Telegram sent by George F. Telfer, May 25,
1898. (OHS collections)

I am on "police" today — so will not have much time to get my shopping done but Povey will look after that.[17] He looks after everything — including my feed.

I am so cold I can't write any more. I could fill a newspaper so far as items — but I can't do the mechanical part.

Will send a postal daily until we start.

Affectionately,
George

« 3 »

Presidio, Cal.
May 22, 1898

Dear Lottie,

Your letter of the 19th just received. Have just returned from our ship — the *Australia* where I am assisting Knapp in the QM Department.[18] Our supplies are being put on board and we have orders to leave camp at 8 A.M. Tuesday.

People here say we have the best ship of the fleet. Mr. Reed has made the trip to Honolulu several times on her and says she is fine. She is steel and fitted up in modern shape — electric lights, baths — even a telephone. Bunks have been put in for the men between decks. Everything is painted white and smells sweet and nice. The officers have a large upper deck covered with an awning. We will take steamer chairs. People say we will want to sleep in them when we strike the tropics. The remark was made yesterday that we are going to make history. If we get away on time — we will be the first American troops to cross the sea — and aside from the invasion of Mexico — the first to land on foreign soil.[19] As our steamer is the fastest, we will doubtless reach Manila first.

The *Charleston* sailed out this morning.[20] She goes to clear the track for us. Our boys lined the shore and cheered as she passed the camp — and she blew her whistle. She is not the *Charleston* you saw. She is stripped of all ornamental work and painted a dull lead color instead of white.

Camped out at the Presidio—San Francisco, July 1898. (OHS neg. 77381)

I shall be glad to get away from here. It is *horrible*. The wind blows most of the time and sand does not hold tent pegs. When it rains, the wet seeps through under the tents and makes it very uncomfortable. Wells, Povey, and I are messing ourselves.[21] We have a box for a table and sit on anything. Last night we got some folding stools and are more comfortable. But fried eggs—brought from the cook tent—a block away—on a tin plate—in a wind are not appetizing.

I see by the papers that Mrs. Reeve came out with her husband and will summer at Los Angeles.[22] Minneapolis gave their regiment a complete outfit of tents. The State, a complete uniform for each man, and Jim Hill deposited $7500.00 to their credit at Hong Kong.[23] Oh! Oregon!

One of the California officers called on us yesterday—(artillery)—he says it is a good thing that we are going with their troops as we will have to act as Wet Nurse. People here are disgusted with their own regiment when placed by side of Oregon. The Nebraska troops are here without uniforms or rifles. Their officers are ignorant of everything military.

Monday night "Taps"

Took dinner with the Raleighs tonight.[24] Sat at table until 9 P.M. Just got home. They are all lovely. Three young men take their meals there and Nan is quite attractive — so it makes a lively place to stay.

We have all our stores on board. I have been sorting shoes and underclothing all day. We have our "duck" uniforms for the tropics all ready to issue as soon as we strike warm weather.[25] Gen'l Anderson goes with us.[26] The California troops did not stand the march to the dock at all. They had 40# to pack and it did them up. Their column was all broken and some of their men fainted. Our boys made the march out here — after a hard journey — came into camp as if on parade, and pitched their tents.

Tuesday (Revelle)

Camp is being struck and I am "packed." Waiting for my tent to fall. Can't write much. Look for next letter from Honolulu — about 30 days.

Affectionately,
George

Letter from Grace just Rec'd

«4»

S.S. *Australia*
San Francisco
May 25, 1898

Dear Lottie,

I have arranged with the Crocker-Woolworth National Bank of San Francisco to send you $75.00 per month.[27] This will doubtless be scaled down on first month as there is some uncertainty of date of commencement of pay.

We understand that the bank will mail you a draft. But it may be that you will have to draw on them. In case you do not hear from the bank the first of the month, go to Mr. Newhall and ask him to draw for it.[28] Show him this letter and enclosed blank — which is a copy of draft I have filed with the bank. The balance is to myself. The bank will not advance over 60%. We sail at noon and this will go to the P.O.

My address: Co. L, 2nd Regt Ore. U.S. Volunteers, Philippine Islands via San Francisco. 5¢ postage. The address is the only one we know. I may never get it — but *perhaps*.

Affectionately,
George
(Will write from Honolulu.)

«5»

On board Str *Australia* 3 days out of San Francisco — May 28, 1898[29]
Events Preceding —

— War with Spain declared Apl 24, 1898
— Writer reported for duty with 2nd Oregon volunteers May 2, 1898
— Mustered in May 15, 1898
— Left with Regt for San Francisco May 16
— Arrived Presidio   "   "   "   18
— Embarked on S.S. [*Australia*]   "   24
— Sailed for Philipines 5 p.m.   "   25

Saturday
May 28, 1898

Have been too sick to think of writing before.

We left San F. (the command under Brig. Gen'l Anderson) on three steamers. The *Peking*, *Australia*, and *City of Sydney*.[30] Gen'l Anderson and staff with correspondents of various newspapers being on the *Australia*. The ships are under control of the Navy department. A naval officer accompanies each ship. The senior officer is on the *Peking*. She is therefore designated as the flag ship and has to lead. This retards our progress — as ours is the fast ship of the fleet. The three ships sail in the following order

Distance abreast about 2 miles. Our speed is about 13 knots an hour. Course Southwest. The *Australia* is very narrow and rolls fearfully. Owing to the fact that the Staff and correspondents take up all the first class state room, the line officers are below in second cabin — 3 in a room. We dress according to seniority — that is, the second Lieutenant dresses first — then the first, then the Captain. Captain Wells and Lt. Povey are with me. Our 1st Sgt. Q.M. Sgt., Clerk and "*Striker*" have the room next.[31] On account of going into the tropics we have chosen an inside room as it is cooler than one next [to] the side of the ship. As this room is quite dark, I do not go inside any oftener than I can help. I purchased a deck chair in San F. The officers have a space reserved for them on one side of the deck and we take our chairs up there and sit and talk all day. The saloon is our assembly room and we have very jolly evenings. We have a piano, banjo, and mandolin for instrumental music. We have considerable vocal talent. Card playing is of course popular.

The reading matter sent from Portland is on tables on one side of the Saloon and the men are allowed to take what they please.

Maj. Eastwick is in command of troops on the *Sidney*.[32] He wanted me to go with him as Quartermaster. It would have been very pleasant — but the *Australia* will land her troops first as the general [Anderson] wants to be first on shore. His uncle was Maj. Anderson of Ft. Sumpter, he himself was the first federal officer to cross the Potomac during the Civil War, and he wants the distinction of landing

Major P. G. Eastwick, of the 3rd Batt., 2nd Oregon Volunteer Infantry. (OHS neg. 77388)

first on foreign soil. If there is to be a fight I want to see it. So I prefer to stay with my company.

My stay in San Francisco was so rushed that I made no calls. My friend Reed hunted me up for dinner. Mrs. Raleigh sent Harry out after me and filled me up to the neck with good things. One of her boarders took me to lunch the next day and I had a

"French" dinner. Mrs. Darling and husband (Converse Darling) came to the Steamer to say goodbye. I had a long talk with her.

Fred is out of prison and supposed to be in South Africa.

Mrs. Raleigh came on board also. She thinks as much of our family as though she belonged to it. I want Grace to visit her.[33] Her children are lovely.

The San Francisco people gave us a great send off. Their own regiment went on board the *Peking* the day before we embarked — but the crowd was as great when we marched down. The Oregon people present made all the noise they could. We were well treated all the time we were there. When we went on board we received a great deal of attention from the ladies. As our men marched up the gang plank in single file — young ladies kissed them goodbye — *Officers were not included.*

Before we raised our anchors various tugs and steamers brought crowds of people out to pelt us with fruit, sing to us, and cheer. While many bands filled the air with music. When we moved down the bay — every sort of steam craft escorted us to the "bar." Yards were manned, color dipped and whistles blew. It was glorious.

We are now getting into warmer latitudes. We sit on deck without overcoats. The sea is "hilly" but there is no wind. Two Albatross have followed us so far. Also a few small birds. The *Peking* has just closed up to hailing distance and the men are hollering at each other.

9

Sunday
May 29, 1898
1150 miles from San F.

Weather is clear and mild. Sea quite smooth. Chaplain held service on upper deck at 2 P.M.[34] Subject of discourse, duty. He advises—1st Duty to self. 2nd Duty to comrades. 3rd Duty to Commanding officer. 4th Duty to parents and wives at home. 5th Duty to God. 6th Duty to country.

Canvas bath tub fixed up on deck for men to bathe. This is a square tub made of sail cloth and large enough for 10 men. Sea water is pumped in constantly—and allowed to run out—so that clean water is always used. The water is warm enough to make bathing in the open air very comfortable. Being no ladies on board, the men do not have to worry over costume. The men have not been receiving their full ration and have suffered in consequence. The Commissary undertook to feed them and it looks as though he expected to make a little something. The Captains (yesterday) called the Colonel's attention to the regulations governing the matter and asked to have a mess officer detailed to superintend the cooking. Capt. Wells was detailed and took charge at once. The result is the men are feeling better today.

Made run of 310 miles from noon yesterday up to noon today.

Measles have broken out again. Fear we shall be quaranteened at Honolulu. Surgeons commence vacinating tomorrow.

Hot bread issued this A.M.—for the first time.

Troops bathing on troopship *Australia.* (From *Harper's,* July 16, 1898.)

Monday
May 30, 1898
1459 miles from San F.

Have just finished first inspection of arms. It was somewhat of a gymnastic exercise. First you jab the bayonet into the deck above. Then you whack the head of the nearest man. You raise the muzzle to

10

your eye to look at inside of barrel and the ship gives a lurch which sends you to the side.

Inspected quarters at 9 A.M. Worse than a visit to China town. Chinamen have more cubic air space.

Body lice have made appearance on men.

Kerrigan — the high jumper — laid up with appendicitis is better.[35] A flying fish landed on deck this morning.

Sea water shows temperature of 65°. Want thin clothing tomorrow. Find that we failed to execute all the papers necessary for drawing our pay in San F. Have got to mail some back from Honolulu. Am very sorry on account of delay in getting money home. Trust you will get Mr. Newhall to write Crocker-Woolworth. They will inform you of the situation. We get no pay ourselves until sometime in July. Only one more blunder on the part of the powers that be.

We expect to land about 8 miles from Manila and camp until reinforcements come. Our command is too small to hold the city. This will allow us to rest until cool weather.

Have got over my sea sickness and am in that contented languid state — where I am satisfied to sit and look at the water all day. I do not even read. My belt will lap twice around me.

There is some talk of touching at Hong Kong for orders. If we do I will cable to you. If not, will try and cable from Manila.

Weather much warmer. Had our first muster this A.M. Men being vacinated. A few more cases of measles. My appetite on increase.

Friends at home would have difficulty in recognizing their boys now. Worn and soiled clothes. Sunburnt and dirty skins. Hunger has destroyed all vestage of good manners. They grab food and devour it in a way that would shock a hobo. The decks are so crowded they can't sit down — on the ground even. Most of them stand and eat as best they can. But with it all they keep their good humor. The ship's officers say they are the most patient lot of men they ever saw. As usual the man from a refined home is the most patient of all. The only trouble we have had has been with country boys — who never knew good homes. We are all believers in Kipling's saying that the best army is an army of gentlemen.

The *New York Herald* correspondent has been amusing us today — making pencil sketches of officers. He gets up some wonderful likenesses. The other correspondents use cameras. He can sketch as fast as an ordinary man writes.

Oregon is censured for sending her troops into the field so poorly equipped. Somebody will hear from it, if these men live to get home. We officers left San F. broke. We will have to pay the steamship at least $30.00 each — for our subsistence, and live for a month after we reach our destination. Of course we *can't* pay. The paymaster does not come out until the next ship. Our families will receive money long before we will. We have the satisfaction of knowing that there are a lot of us and we can pretty near terrorize any community if we are not cared for.

I will send you a few sweet pea blossoms with this. They are a part of the bouquet I carried on the march to the steamer at San F. I never did such a thing before — but a young man came out from the crowd and handed the bunch to me. They were pretty and the thought came to me that they would serve as a memento — so I carried them in my sword hand most of the way. Afterwards I put them in my belt. They were eagerly sought for by San F. ladies, and I was glad I had them to give.

We expect to overtake the *Charleston* at Honolulu. She is to convoy us the remainder of the way. As she is much slower than we are — our progress will be slow.

The ships officers have run a steam pipe into an empty water tank and we are having the men put their soiled clothes into it and steaming them for 2 hours. Then taking them into the cold bath and rinsing. We *think* this may destroy the vermin.

May [June] 1, 1898
In sight Sandwich Islands

First land sighted about noon. Men all delighted.

The measels have gained — rather than lost — so there is a chance of our not going ashore. It will be pretty tough as we need many things from stores.

Officers are showing up with white collars on. Naval and ship's officers have white duck clothes.

Hawaii Annexation Day, August 12, 1898. Telfer mentions meeting white-bearded Sanford B. Dole in Letter 8. (OHS neg. 77498)

Will close this now in order to have it ready to mail if I find we are going to be short of time. Will send more if I have a chance.

Geo. F. Telfer

« 6 »

Honolulu,
June 3, 1898

Dear Family,

We sail from here at 7 A.M. tomorrow. Mail arrived tonight and I expected a letter — but none came. I sent a letter to Willis today — written at the Palace.[36] I think I dated it wrong.

This is as near paradise as any place I expect to see on this earth. Will write descriptions when under way. The Pearsons met me at the dock and entertained me every moment of yesterday.[37] Today the men were banqueted by the citizens. This place raised $100,000.00 for entertainment. We have been feasted and entertained until we are crazy. I lunched today with the Humphreys. Mrs. Humphrey is a sister of Mrs. Whithead — the Chinese lady who married the naval officer and created such a sensation a year ago. Her father was Chinese Minister here. She has some of the look of a Japanese. She is very much of a lady. They entertain very lavishly.

The people here are largely American. Your old friend Bierbach waited on me in a drug store today and I meet many that I knew.[38]

I wish you could see the palms. And I have sampled so many kinds of fruit that I have become hopelessly confused.

We will leave here dressed in white duck — *including shoes*. This is the regular costume here.

The people are crazy for annexation. They have furnished us with coal and allowed us to land our troops and parade. This means that the U.S. will have to establish a protectorate or the powers will gobble the Islands.

Many things are cheap here. My white uniform made like my blue and trimmed with the white braid — cost $5.25.[39] My white canvas shoes, $1.50. Of course imported articles are high.

The *Charleston* moves so slow that we expect to be 25 days getting to Manila. Address letter to Co. L, 2nd Oregon U.S. Volunteers, Philippine Expedition via San Francisco. I am eating hearty and enjoying myself. The days are hot — but nights are cool. I mailed account of trip written from day to day — and it may interest you. The newspapers will all have letters written from here.

Love to all.
Affectionately
George

13

Boys entering the palace grounds in Hawaii. (From *On to Manila*)

Honolulu, H.I.
May [June 3] 6 1898

Dear Willis,

This letter is written [on Senate Chamber station-ary] in the Senate Chamber of the Hawaiian Republic. It is one of the rooms in which the late queen was kept a prisoner. The building was her palace.

From the windows we look down upon our entire command — being fed by the citizens of Honolulu. They are eating more kinds of fruit than I ever heard of. Tables are spread on the grass under the trees. One tree shades a whole regiment.

We have just had our pictures taken on the veranda — will try and have one sent.

Affectionately your father,
Geo. F. Telfer
1st Lt. 2nd Or. Volunteers USA
Philippine Expedition

S.S. *Australia*.
June 6, 1898

We sailed from Honolulu Saturday morning under convoy of *Charleston*. Our course was due west — following 20th parallel north. Lat. On Sunday the commander of the *Charleston* signaled that his order was to proceed to the Ladrone islands to capture one of them and destroy two Spanish gunboats (or capture them).[40] He said it would delay him about two days. The rest of his message we could not take it. Our course the naval officer in charge has it — but he don't tell us anything so we can only form conjectures. We hope we will be allowed near enough to see the scrap. I don't think troops will be landed — from this expedition at least. Before this reaches you, the world will know the result. And we may be blown up. But you may imagine we are in a state of expectancy. Our course changed yesterday and we are sailing southwest.

Life is somewhat monotonous. Like Mark Twain's diary — we get up — eat — go to bed.[41] At noon we (the steamers) close in for signals. We have several on board who can read the "wigwag".[42] We "take off" the signals and translate when we can. Then we discuss probable movement until we get tired. Then we sit in a row and look at the ocean — read a *little* — talk or sleep. It is very hot and we wear duck clothes most of the time. The meal hours are all welcome. In the evening we sing some.

Of course we have some duties. I am in command

Troops being fed in Hawaii. (From *On to Manila*)

of Co. L and both Wells and Povey are on detached duty. This relieves me from guard duty. I have to superintend company mess and inspect quarters, and look after discipline as well as I can. The men are idle — uncomfortable, and inclined to be unruly. The food provided is not adapted to the tropics. The men understand that their officers cannot help matters but they are hungry just the same. We are all homesick for Honolulu. We each of us had the best two days we ever knew. If a common, dirty soldier happened to stop in front of some elegant home to admire it — the occupants rushed out and invited him in. He was fed and entertained as long as he remained. We officers were not allowed to even walk. Carriages were called up to take us any place we mentioned — and one or two gentlemen accompanied us. Business houses were all closed — except Chinese. When we left, the ladies followed the native custom of placing a wreath of flowers — called "leis" around the neck of every soldier. These are ropes of flowers — usually carnations strung on cocoanut fibers and long enough to pass over the head and hang around the neck. The fiber is passed through the flower. A guest at dinner is usually decorated this way. It is a very pretty custom. Mrs. Pearson gave me one at a dinner made of red and white carnations — a stranger gave me one on ship board. I wish I could send them home — but they would not keep.

I was presented to the president — he is very much of a gentleman.[43] The queen's old palace is used by the Hawaiian National Guard as a club house. All during our stay lunch was spread there — day and night. Beer and wine was passed constantly and committees were on hand to see that we were entertained. Our troops were given unlimited liberty — and behaved as well as though on the streets of Portland. The Californians were not given leave — but were marched around in squads. They are a tough lot. The resident Oregonians were proud of their state and yelled themselves hoarse whenever we appeared.

The senate was in session one day while we were there. When the session opened the Chaplain prayed for the success of our mission — a remarkable proceeding in a foreign legislative body. Papers will doubtless be sent you from Honolulu giving account of proceedings.

We are running very slow — not much more than half speed. These large steel ships do not tremble under motion of engines as river steamers. Consequently we hardly know when we are in motion. We roll fearfully and if any of us sit near an open port we are apt to get a ducking.

Thursday
June 9, 1898

Tomorrow is the day we lose. We jump from Thursday to Saturday. There will be no Friday.

The only thing we see of interest are the flying fish.[44] These we see singly and in schools. Most writers on natural history state that the flying fish does not fly — just makes jumps from wave to wave. This is wrong. These fish fly quite long distances — turning repeatedly in their flight. They keep near the water, however. They look very pretty.

Sunday
June 12, 1898

We lost the 10th and jumped to 11th. We celebrated the crossing of the 180th degree longitude. last night after naval form. At officers mess — dinner — each glass was filled with champaign, we drank — standing — "Sweethearts and Wives". You will perhaps remember that all naval officers drink this toast when they cross 180° — longitude — It might seem a very slight affair to read about.[45] But out here in this vast expanse of water, *so* far from every body we love — it is very solem. Someone tried to throw merriment into the ceremony by adding the sentiment — *"Hoping they may never meet."*

After dinner we adjourned to the deck — the band was brought. Also what musical talent we have — a wash boiler full of claret punch was brewed and we had a jolly evening. At midnight we adjourned to the bathing tank and let the hose play on us. The water — pumped in a constant stream from the ocean is now 85° degrees temperature. As we are never cool day or night — you can imagine how delightful it is to stand waist deep in a tank of water with a 2 inch stream playing on you. It is a sea bath without the discomforts of tramping through the sand and wind. Today, being Sunday, the Colonel ordered an inspection of arms. When one considers that we nearly die for want of occupation during the week, and that Sunday is a day of rest, also the War Department forbids Sunday inspections — one cannot help wondering what this work was put on us for.

We are now in that part of the Pacific Ocean known as the *Doldrums*. It is understood that it always rains here. This morning we watched a shower come up from the east and 15 minutes later one came from the west. However, the sun shines constantly — during the day. There is no wind. This is fortunate — for if the wind should blow — it would be hotter still and the seas would drive us from the deck, oblige us to close all portholes and suffocate between decks. We are about half way between Honolulu and Guam (one of the Ladrone islands which we are expected to capture). We are sailing near the 16th parallel. One mile south of us is the *City of Peking*, 1/2 to 1 mile ahead and 1/2 mile to the south is the *Charleston* — dark — grim — silent — *ugly* — setting our pace and course. Where she leads — we follow. The *Sidney* is a little to the rear and north of us. We never approach near enough to hear each other's bands playing. It seems very unsocial.

Discipline is somewhat slack on board, and some of the officers feel very much dissatisfied. In case of an alarm, a panic might ensue which would endanger the safety of the ship. It is customary on shipboard to drill troops on going to quarters. This prepares them for emergencies. The company officers understand this — but are powerless to put the system into force.

Gen'l Anderson is observing officers closely and doubtless forming his own opinions. He asks many questions and has long talks with company commanders. The old troubles — two factions — will result.

Thursday
June 16, 1898
10:10 P.M. Lat 14° N, Course West

Events are not numerous. We are pretty busy —
with schools, inspections, etc. We have reveille at
6 A.M. I have to be up for that. Then sit around until
8 for breakfast. Then inspection of quarters. Then a
lecture one hour long. This runs us to noon. After
dinner we read — except those who instruct non com
school. We have to attend retreat roll call and officers
school at 8 P.M.

After 10 o'clock we all go out and soak in the big
tub. The *Charleston* signaled us about an hour ago
and got us very much worked up. But when it was
translated it read "Hope all are well on board ship."

Cardwell signaled from the *Sidney* today that he
had removed a dangerous appendix from a man on
board and that his patient was doing well.[46]

It is very warm. And that peculiar heat that is
found only in greenhouses — very damp. If one walks
across the deck they perspire. If you *don't* perspire —
you will be sick. And then think of having to drink
water 85°. There is no wind. The smoke from the
stacks raises straight up. We see no ships. We are out
of the world and we all wonder what you will think
when we are not reported from any place. We run at
half speed and change our course frequently. This
will tend to mislead any ships sent to intercept us.
Ordinarily we would be at the Philippines now. As it
is, we are not likely to get there until July.

Saturday
June 18, 1898

Yesterday was an eventful day. The fleet "laid to"
and the *Charleston* had target practice with big guns
for two hours. A floating target was put out and she
moved about and fired from different positions. We
would first see a burst of smoke — then a splash of
water a mile away — then a deafening crash followed
by a second. Then when we looked toward the
Charleston she was completely obscured by smoke.
This was repeated at each shot. The commander of
the fleet — Capt. Glass, and the naval officers in
charge of the *Peking* and *Sidney* came on board to
consult with Gen'l Anderson regarding operations.[47]
Beyond the fact that several bottles of champaign
were conveyed to the council chamber — we have
heard nothing.

It was a relief to lay still as a refreshing breeze was
blowing — which we cannot feel when running before it.

I tried sleeping on deck last night — but a rain
storm at midnight drove me below. We sighted land —
north of us this morning. It was an Island with an
unpronounceable name laying east of the Ladrone
group.

Monday
June 20, 1898

Today we captured the Island of Guam — and are
now peacefully anchored in its harbor — and wishing

19

we could go somewhere else. We always want to go some place else.

We sighted the land at sunrise. Rain and fog shut out the shore — so we cruised around some time before locating the harbor. The *Charleston* finally turned in and we watched operations from outside. We could see one ship — but did not know whether it was a warship or not. The *Charleston* slowly steamed in and we hung over the rail and held our breaths. Pretty soon a line of blue smoke shot out from her forward guns. This was closely followed by another, then another. *Then* we realized that there was a "scrap" on. We afterwards learned that the ship we saw was a Japanese trading vessel and the shots (12 in all) were fired at a mud fort in the harbor. The officers and governor had not heard that war was declared. Naturally they were surprised when the shots fell about their ears. The town is inland, but a man happened to be on the beach with a horse. He went into town with the news and the customs and health officers came down and put off to make the usual examinations. They were somewhat astonished to learn of Dewey's Manila victory. We take coal and go on. I have not heard whether it is intended to leave any troops here or not.

My "vacinate" is working and I feel very badly. Every body is broken out with prickley heat. My body is a sight to behold. Think of sweating all night and all day. It don't just come out on your face — but all over. My pajams have to be hung up to dry in the morning.

The scenery around is beautiful. Great groves of cocoanuts. The island is a volcanic formation and consequently mountainous. The foothills are green like Oregon.

Thursday
May [June] 24, 1898

We left Gaum yesterday at 4 P.M. Tuesday was given over to the surrender. The governor did not come out and *surrender* as told. So instructions were given to send a force ashore after him. The expedition being a naval one, Gen'l Anderson had nothing to do with the matter. But Capt. Glass had only 30 marines. So, he asked Gen'l Anderson to furnish two companies. A and D were assigned. We laid 3 miles from shore and a heavy squall came up. The landing of 200 troops was a problem. Soldiers who thought they could row were detailed as oarsmen. Boats were collected from the entire fleet. It took over two hours to load them. It was blowing so hard that the men could make no headway. So a steam launch took them in tow. The rain came down in torrents and the boats pitched like mad. When the party was within two miles of shore a boat came out and signaled a return. The governor had surrendered and was on his way out. So our soldiers did *not* march up a hill and down again — but sailed away and back again. The Spanish Army — 50 men and 6 officers, The Governor and 3 officials were taken on board the *Sidney*. The stars and stripes were hoisted on fort "Santa Cruz." Guns were fired and bands played. The sun came out and we rejoiced. You will have a full description of the event in the *Oregonian. Harper's Weekly* will have some good sketches. Also the San F.

dailys. *An officer of the Army is not allowed to write much on the conduct of military affairs.* Letters sometimes miscarry, so I make no comments.

I went ashore yesterday morning and visited a native village. The people are of the Mongolian type mixed with Spanish. They talk some English, are cleanly as to person and very friendly. We bought lots of fruit (lemons 12.5 per 100) and some shells. Their houses are — many of them — built of coral rock and whitewashed. They have steep roofs thatched with palm leaves and are very picturesque. They are Roman Catholics and have a quaint little church. The capital city is called Agana. I should like to have gone there but none of us were granted the time.

The man on the *Sidney* whom Cardwell operated on for appendicites died before the ship entered the harbor and was buried at sea. The first death in the expedition.[48] Kerrigan (who was down with the same complaint recovered without operation). One man in Davis' Co. drank too much ice water (having stolen ice from the cold storage) and got his intestines knotted so Ellis cut him open — took out a section of intestine — inserted a silver tube or button and the man is getting along nicely.[49]

We all exchanged visits at Guam and I enjoyed meeting my friends on the *Sidney*. I wish I had been assigned to her. Besides having friends on board, she is not so crowded and has none of the unpleasant features that we have to contend with here.

Saturday
May [June] 25, 1898
Lat 15° 22" north — course west

My vacinate is on the improve and I am feeling better. But oh! the long dreary trip! No change in the weather — the wind blows in one direction always. It is hot day and night. My stomach turns against one-month-old meat and I find little in the eating line that I can enjoy. I have no close friends on board and don't talk. I am suffering from blues and general discomfort. We are so crowded on deck that I can't sit down without some body falling over my feet. It is impossible for me to sleep over 6 hours out of 24 and I feel *mean*.

Tuesday
May [June] 28

We arrived at the extreme northern point of the island of Luzon (Philippine group) today. And met the *Baltimore* — who had been waiting for us for 9 days. The meeting was quite exciting. Of course when we saw smoke we could not tell friend from foe. The ships were quickly formed in column with *Charleston* in lead. Then commenced the maneuvering for position. It was like two game roosters. I was on the bridge of the *Australia* and could see it all plainly. It was very exciting. As soon as each recognized the other we proceeded on our way.

We are anchored tonight under guard of Dewey's fleet and the lights on Manila twinkle in the distance—not much farther than the lights of Portland from our house. Our journey is done—we have seen Dewey and yelled our throats raw. Dewey came on board about 6 o'clock. He looks like his pictures—a small, white whiskered, pleasant gentleman. A campsight will be selected in the morning and it will be then decided how we are to be killed. Manila bay is a magnificent piece of water—many times larger than San Francisco bay and the city is larger than San F.

It is about 20 miles by land from where we are to the city. The land between is low and evidently covered with plantations. The insurgents and natives are fighting all the time and we could see the smoke from a burning village as we came into the bay.

Our trip down the China Sea was awful. We struck a typhoon and executed gymnastics for 48 hours. I had to sleep in my state room last night—or rather, I tried to sleep. I had hard work keeping in I can tell you. Everything that could get loose did so—crashed into everything else. Most of the officers stayed up all night. The *Charleston* afforded us much amusement during the day. She would dip her nose into the water clear back to her mast—then she would raise like a dog and shake herself—the spray would fly as high as her smoke stack.

The correspondents for *New York Sun, Harpers Weekly* and *San Francisco Call* as well as *Oregonian*—will send their letters by this mail and I will not attempt descriptions. The articles in *New York Sun* and *Harpers Weekly* are written by a man named Davis who left the Flying Squadron to join this.[50] They will be the best sent. You can arrange to get the numbers at the news stand. Davis has some excellent photographs, if they come out well. I think the illustrated articles in the *San F. Call* will also be good.

Our dogs are quite well. They were seasick at first—but are all right now. Mike distinguished himself as a ratter and the ships crew make much of him. When the sailors are heaving on ropes he gets ahold and pulls too. But no matter where he is—he answers assembly and mess calls—always taking his place one pace in front of the company.

This letter will go via Hong Kong and Vancouver. A dispatch boat leaves here tomorrow and I am getting it ready for that time. The Associated Press will have cables announcing our arrival so you will know we are safe long before this reaches you. Of course we have not been on shore—but we are all entranced with what we see from shore. We all talk of locating here—if the U.S. holds it. Nearly every country that has a navy is represented here by a warship. Our fleet is on one side of the harbor—the others form one fleet on the other side. Of course they are watching our movements.

The China Sea used to be known as the Yellow Sea, but it is not yellow.

We are all disgusted with being explorers. A plain, simple voyage will do for us. We have knocked around the Pacific Ocean for 36 days. It is too much of a good thing. The voyage can be made in 15.

I hope to get news from home some day — if only an *Oregonian*.

You will doubtless be able to get our address better in Portland than I can give it. But in lieu of anything better, use the one you now have.

With lots of love and good wishes for you all. I remain

Affectionately yours,
George F. Telfer

I am reduced to 25¢ and no prospect of money for several weeks.

Enlisted Men
   June 6
Breakfast
Steak — Boiled Potatoes — Coffee
Dinner
Soup — Boiled Potatoes
   Boiled Onions
   June 7
Breakfast
Rice — Boiled Potatoes — Biscuits
Coffee —
Dinner
Stew — Tea

« 9 »

Cavite P.I.
July 8, 1898

Dear Family,

Newspapers and bulletins doubtless keep you posted somewhat as to the whereabouts of the Philippine Expeditionary Forces. My daily life is the same as that of the balance of the 3,000 — and the only satisfaction we have in having the newspaper correspondents around is that they do our letter writing to a certain extent.

I have stood the climate pretty well. My light weight is in my favor. Today my bowels trouble me a little — for the first time — but not seriously. Everybody catches *that*. I drink nothing but tea and confine myself to bananas for fruit. We are all so indolent that we hate to move. Dr. Cardwell thinks 30 days will see us well acclimated. The men are being worked too hard. All our stores have to be carried from the landing 1/4 mile off (equal to 1 mile at home). The men do all this. The Q.M. Dept. declines to hire the work done. There are no wagons, nor horses and they *"pack"* everything. On this account there has been little in the way of drill. It rains every day — *thunder storms*. We are comfortably housed in barracks built of brick — 150 years old. Each company has a long room to itself. Their bunks are made in the shape of frames about 5 1/2 feet long, panneled with rattan or bamboo. These frames — or cots — are laid on trestles about 18 inches high — and made of iron

First quarters of American soldiers in
Cavite. (OHS neg. 77393)

(look like andirons). Some cots are wide enough for
2 — and some for 1 man. I have one of the rattan
ones. These were of course left by the Spaniards.
And as a Spaniard is a short man — of course my feet
project. I cannot get used to laying next the rattan —
as do the natives. So I have a piece of cotton cloth
under me. I have my mosquito bar on wires over my
head, and a sheet over my feet. Some of our officers
suffer terribly from mosquito bites, but strange to say
they do not poison me.

We officers have the second floor of a building
near the sea wall — overlooking the bay toward the
Manila shore. There are 3 rooms connected, open
onto a corridor on 1 side and an enclosed veranda on
the other. All of our regiment are in the one suite of

rooms and we are uncomfortably crowded. We eat
and sleep in the same rooms. When we get up in
the morning — (4:30) we most of us stand our cots
against the wall in order to make room for tables to
eat off of. We have one advantage — a breeze comes
up from the bay every afternoon and blows across
and through our rooms. Some nights we need the
covering of a blanket.

Within pistol shot of our windows are the remains
of most of the Spanish Warships which Dewey sunk.
I never realized what a tremenduous victory it was.
13 steel ships destroyed.[51] We are on the point of a
peninsula and the insurgents occupy the ground between us and the Spanish line. So we do not perform
outpost duty. The Spanish and insurgents sleep all
day and commence fighting about 9 or 10 at night.
Two hours generally ends the engagement. We can
hear all the noise but the vegetation is too dense to
allow us to see. We think nothing of it anyhow. Those
who are reading look up at the first cannon shot —
then go on reading. The sound is something like
hearing China New Years at home. The cannon is a
little louder than a bomb. The musketry sounds like
fire-crackers. The insurgents are composed of the
original native population.[52] Their General Agua-
naldo is an able man — but his troops are a scattered
mob.[53] They seem to have no system of formation.
They are very friendly with us *now* — but we will
have to whip them — if we intend to hold the islands.
We fear them more than we do the Spanish. When we
walk through the streets — day or night — we have
our revolvers in our belts under our hands ready for
quick action.

I wish you could all see this quaint old city — 350 years old. It is a walled town and built entirely of brick. The town we occupy was built and occupied by the Spanish. It is connected with the old native village by a causeway one mile long. The old village is built of bamboo and very picturesque. Our barracks are between the new city and the navy yard — a modern affair occupying the point outside the wall. It is a finer equipped yard than can be found in the U.S. The buildings are elegant. The machinery of late pattern and complete. The offices and quarters — palaces with tile floors, and furnished with the most elegant modern furniture. Of course when the Spanish evacuated the place, it was looted by natives. Elegant desks and chests were burst open to get at contents. If we could have been here to have saved property, it would have been a rich haul. Now we see native hucksters selling fruit, etc. displayed on mahogany library tables. And native officers wearing diamond rings.

There are several thousand Spanish prisoners around town. They are a very insignificant, lifeless lot of men. Their methods of fighting are obsolete. They depend upon volley firing — solid masses of troops — use sword and bayonet, etc. I think they would surrender Manila on demand — if Dewey could guarantee protection of life and property of residents. As it is they are afraid that the insurgents and usual criminal class will loot the place. A city of 350,000 population cannot be guarded by 3,000 men — at time of war. We hope terms will be made as soon as the second expedition arrives. We came to take Manila and are fretting under inaction.

General Emilio Aguinaldo. (From *On to Manila*)

Oh dear! I wish I could get a letter from home. A newspaper would be better than nothing. Not one word direct or indirect since leaving San F. Some of us are very homesick. A soldier has more time to think than the business man — and consequently his family is in his mind oftener. Perhaps the soldier's love for family is no more sincere — but it is certainly more apparent. I have the two lieutenants from Co. H [54] in my room and so hear much of Grace's crowd. [55] The Pratt boys [56] take the hard fare and treatment like men and not like the *down trodden working gentleman.*

The Albany company are near us and I pass through their quarters frequently. They stand the racket in good shape.

We take one dollar in American money (provided you can borrow one) and change it for two Spanish dollars. This seems nice—but you can buy twice as much for an American dollar as you can for a Spanish dollar.

The Spanish houses and stores in Cavite were of course abandoned by their owners and preempted by natives. Consequently there are no stores—except fruit and vegetable dealers and a few dealers in native fabrics. We can't buy anything except at military depot. This does not help us out on many things.

We three officers—combine on one servant. This small Malay struggles through life with the name of Juan Secondora. He don't know a word of English. When we converse with him we send for an interpreter. I have a list of words to use in case of emergency.

I was sorry to find that my photograph case did not contain the last pictures of the children. I think I must have taken them out to show and neglected to return them. Have them ready to send when you can be sure of an address. We learn that there is to be a mail out tomorrow, so I will proceed to close.

In my next I will try and give some description of manners, customs, etc. I will try and get some

Willis Glaze Telfer, second from top.
(Author's collection)

sketches made. Postage being high—and I can't get thin paper—I must condense my letters.

Affectionately,
Geo. F. Telfer

26

Cavite P.I.
Jul. 18, 1898

Dear Willis,

Your letter of May 18 reached me (via) U.S.S. transport *China* — yesterday. You must know that it was a very welcome letter. It seems ages since I heard from my boy. And I am glad to know that he is taking an active part in the proceedings of his fellows. You are one of a small republic now. Your actions are mostly "play." But as you play now — so you will act when older. *"Men are but boys grown old."* I hear and see war every day — but it seems no more to me than the play of boyhood. Always be one of the crowd — when wrong is not the objective. Accustom youself to the ways of your associates — not with the idea of imitating — but that you may know how to influence them to act as you wish. Above all — act *right* — put aside all that is vulgar — rude — or mean.

This document is taken from the Archives to the Spanish Navy Yard at Cavite.[57] Tons of them are thrown about. We use the tin boxes in which they were filed for bread boxes. We find the paper very handy. Some documents date back in the last century.

I wish you could see some of the wonderful things here. I must answer Grace's letter — so will close.

Your affectionate father,
Geo F. Telfer

Cavite P.I.
July 18, 1898

Dear Daughter Grace,

I received your nice letter of May 29 yesterday — when the second expedition arrived (Steamer *China*).[58] It was the first news from home. We understand that their is a lot of mail at Hong Kong, but we have no way of getting it. When the ships of the second expedition were sighted day before yesterday we were much excited. We looked for letters — and money. We got some letters — but our money did not come — so we are still dead broke — but happy. (Just saw Martin Pratt — he said he felt better, had six letters.) We hope that the arrival of more troops means a move on Manila at once. We are suffering from inaction, and the prize is so near.

A week ago Sunday, Capts. Wells, Heath, Prescott and myself, with one man as orderly, and escorted by Capt. Juan Arivelo — Aguinaldo's chief of staff — made a trip to Pasig — 8 miles in the rear of Manila.[59] On the way we passed closer to the fighting lines and looked down into the city. We were the first Americans ever seen in the city of Pasig, and created great excitement. The natives are much impressed by our size. None of them are over five feet in height, and slender in proportion. Capt. Heath is 6 feet and weighs about 180. Capt. Prescott is not so tall, but heavy. Wells is short and I am myself. They thought I must come from another part of the U.S. The people are very kind hearted and like to entertain us. They

Buying fish on a Pasig River beach. (OHS neg. 77366)

are very neat — but do not use knives and forks nor even chop sticks. So we do not enjoy eating with them as much as we might. Still, I have sampled their food. They place a platter of rice on the table and each person takes a wad of it in his hand — rolls it in a dish of fish oil — and conveys it to the mouth. They also eat a small fish — like a minnow — raw — dried in the sun. The higher class, of course, do not eat this way. We were entertained by Capt. Arivelos mother at Pasig. They are refugees from Manila and people of importance. They were short of furniture — but had complete table service. They have great variety of dishes and season highly. They use considerable garlic — but not much red pepper. I like their food very much. They do not use much liquor. A little brandy is taken at times — but in very small quantity. Their manners are enough of the latin race to be pleasing — but backed by greater depth of feeling which makes you like them. They are very fond of music. Even the poorer class have pianos and play well. The lower class play the harp, mandolin, violin, and guitar. Every place we go instruments are brought out and we hear "After the Ball", "Ta ra ra boom de lay", etc. — as well as "Blue Danube", "Maidens Prayer", "Travitore", etc. Some of them are really fine performers. Unlike the Hawaiians — they have no native airs. The Roman Catholic church considered the native music profane — and as the church ruled in these parts, the music was changed. The opera house in Manila has been closed since the blockade on account of general poverty — but I presume a company will be brought over when we get in. Italian is the usual nationality.

The article in June *McClure* gives a very fair description of the country, but is evidently written from memory and slurred. I have not written much myself as I knew there would be some good descriptions soon.

One thing worthy of note is the fact — that although this is a tropical climate, that Spain has given it to the church to misrule for 350 years, that the people have been thrown in contact with the seafaring people of other lands — with all this her population is 8,000,000 — only one hundredth part of which is foreign, and the mixed bloods are confined to this Island. And this population is as perfect in physique as any race I have seen. The men are short — but deep chested and broad shouldered. They are quick of thought and action — not dull and stupid as expected in such climates. If you will investigate statistics bearing on Cuba you will find that the native race is about extinct, and the so called Cuban is a mixture of races. The same applys to South and Central America. But this race of square head, copper colored little men has held its own.

The women are the heads of families. They earn most of the money and boss the ranch. They carry every thing — from an orange to a 150# basket of fish — on their heads. They wear a wooden soled slipper — with toe cover and no heel. They walk from the waist down — swinging the arms. They keep the slipper on by the action of the great toe. When you see them barefooted and with no head burden, they look very funny. They wiggle their bodies and spread raise the great toe, but hold the head erect and neck rigid. They chew the betel nut and it stains their teeth red and causes decay.[60] They all watch us and want to imitate our ways. They are fast discarding the betel nut on account of the effect on teeth. Dentists do a fine business in Manila.

Wells and I take long strolls into the country and visit the natives — for the purpose of studying their language and customs. Wells is very apt at language and can hold quite lengthy conversations. I am very

"They [the women] carry every thing — from an orange to a 150# basket of fish — on their heads." Letter 10. (OHS neg. 77384)

dull at language and don't catch it. The natives want to learn English — so it will not be long until one can make their wants known all over.

We suffer for water more than anything else. We have to boil rain water for drinking purposes. Having no ice to cool it with — you can imagine it is *not* like Bull Run. We don't dare eat the fruit on account of bowel trouble. So we drink tea, coffee, and chocolate. Eat prunes and canned peaches and pears. We have too much sickness — but only one death since starting. The Expedition which arrived yesterday had 5. Our Medical Department is earning great praise. Each doctor takes as much pains with a sick man as though it was private practice. We have very few sick enough to stay in hospital.

The most disagreeable thing to contend with is the crowded quarters (for officers). "Familiarity breeds contempt" is a popular saying — applied to men — but when you take a jumble of men, beds, toilet articles, soiled clothing, and provisions all mixed up in small rooms, you realize how much truth there is in the saying. We live in hopes of getting to Manila — and proper quarters. The Colorado and Pennsylvania troops are being landed today. They don't come here but are being landed in position near Manila. The supposition is that we will be landed with the regulars under the guns of Dewey's fleet — *in* the city. The fact that the California troops have gone and we are here with the regulars, and it is supposed the attack is to be made so soon leads us to accept the theory, anyhow. We don't want to camp — that is in a large camp. It is sure death to sleep on the ground.[61] A native will not sit down on the ground for a short rest. You have a bamboo platform built about 4 feet high. It is too hot to sleep in tents — so you have to build a hut of palms. All this can be done for a small detachment but not for a large body.

We do not look for much fighting. In fact I don't think the Spanish soldiers *will* fight. The prisoners are such puny looking little monkeys. Stoop shouldered, white, and lifeless. There are 2,000 loose around town and we have acquired great contempt for the outfit.

We mess with Co. H officers. Povey is mess officer. One of the cooks that used to be at The Portland is cook.[62] One "striker" and one native wait on us. We have a folding camp table and Co H have a small table which they place with ours. We have blue and white enamel ware and each man his knife, fork and spoons. For food we depend upon canned goods mostly. It is all good with exception of butter. This is somewhat oily. It is so hot that canned corn beef dries up in cans.

The chaplain has found a piano and placed it in our hallway downstairs. Every man who feels so inclined drums on it until we are about crazy.

We have recieved files of the *Oregonian* up to June 13. The old controversy over silver vs. gold seems very much of a chestnut to us, and home life seems very "hum drum."

This letter will be hard to read — but it may amuse you figuring it out. I will close with lots of love to all.

Your affectionate father,
Geo. F. Telfer

Looking toward Manila from top of Fort Malate. (OHS neg. 77363)

« 12 »

Cavite P.I.
July 24, 1898
Sunday night

Dear Lottie,

Tattoo has just sounded and one more dreary — lonesome day is at an end — nearly. I *can* stand 4 days of the week for we *do* have one hour's drill in the morning and another at night. But Saturday and Sunday we cannot even drill. It has rained so that walking was not pleasant — so I have chafed and fretted for two days. Our daily life consists in getting up at 4:30 A.M. — Men's breakfast, 5. Drill 6 to 7 — Officers breakfast. Guard mount at 8 — if you are fortunate enough to come on for duty. Inspection of

Canal around Manila. (OHS neg. 77367)

quarters 9. Dinner 12–1. Drill 4. Retreat 6:30. Supper 7. Men are not allowed out of quarters from 10:30 A.M. to 3:30 P.M. They are supposed to sleep. We are not allowed to drill our companies at any time — except as specified. We are not allowed to go beyond a certain line — 4 miles out. So, the men lay around and get discontented. The officers — crowded into quarters too small for them — with no privacy — quarrel with each other or play poker all day. We do not even have the novelty of camp. We cannot bathe — for the bathroom has to be used for a mess room, and water is scarce. We take out tin wash basins and a rag and jostle one another while making a pretense of washing our sweaty bodies. We cannot go into the sea water on account of poisonous fish.[63] Cavite is held by us and the buildings are all aban-

33

doned by owners. Every officer might have at least one room — a building if necessary — but no — we are herded like emigrants. We are Volunteers — under regular army officers who are bound to break us up if they can. We have had no pay since enrollment, and are penniless — so cannot buy things to make our lot endurable. Everything is expensive. Bannanas cost nearly as much as in Portland. The native is a shrewd trader and knows that he must make the best of his chance.

The other troops have all been put in tents across the bay near the insurgents. They have outposts — pickets, etc. — so life is not a burden to them. The regulars are with us of course — also, Gen'l Tommy [Thomas M. Anderson]. The supply depot is in our charge and we are highly honored — but we did not enlist to sit around a hot room all day. I will give the General credit for wanting to take Manila at once. But Dewey ranks him and will not cooperate until Gen'l Merritt arrives.[64]

We walk over to the wall or out on the water front every evening and watch the electric lights of Manila — "so near and yet so far." We can almost see the people. We are told of hotels, club houses, brewerys, ice machines, cafes, and all luxuries of the large city — all within reach — when Dewey gives the word. People from there say that the city will be surrendered on demand. It would be offered now — but the Gov. Gen'l knows it means death when he reaches Spain.

Everybody says I am very much improved in appearance. I feel well and eat lots. I have walked 10 miles in the heat of the day — and felt none the worse for it. But most of the officers knock out. They don't stand the climate as well as I do.

This is a good country for men. The married man seems to take care of the children and promenade around in spotless, starched white clothes. The women wash and run fruit stands. They are devoted to each other and the children. Never were babies and children made so much of. I looked at one family group on a boat today — (Boat people live on their boats — are born and grow up there). The wife was sitting on the floor, the husband laid with his head in her lap, and the baby in his arms. The wife was engaged in hunting vermin which seemed to have lodged in his head. It was a picture of domestic bliss.

When you purchase another mosquito net for a man who is going to a mosquito country, remember to get it large enough. I have sewed pieces of sheeting on to piece it out. The camphor ice is fine for allaying the itching.[65] We do not have fleas. The red ant is troublesome. We never lay on the ground. Dining tables stand with the four legs in cups of water to prevent the ants walking off with the food.

Monday
July 25, 1898

The ordinary means of transit is a covered cart — much like the one used in Japan — only those are drawn by man power — while these are drawn by very small ponies. The driver sits on a board which crosses the rig where the dash board usually is. He puts his feet on the cross bar. The natives being low of stature, the cover of the cart is low — so that we

Filipino women washing clothes in the Pasig River. (OHS neg. 77383)

cannot sit in them with hats on. When seated, the driver hollers at his small pony and it lights out on a gallop. These ponies are as small as those seen in circuses. They do not stand higher than my arm pit. The whole outfit is very funny.

The women take great pride in their hair. It is very long and wavy. They comb it whenever they have an idle moment.

Gen'l Merritt arrived today. Also a Pay Master. Also some mail. None of these have come ashore yet — so we don't know much. There is mail to Hong Kong tomorrow and I may get this off . . . .

Affectionately yours,
George

On August 13, 1898, Capt. Harry L. Wells led the 2nd Oregon Volunteer Infantry Co. L. through the Luneta Gate (in the three hundred year-old great wall around Manila); the company was to act as provost guard. (OHS neg. 77443)

« 13 »

Cavite P.I.
July 30, 1898

Dear Lottie,

Nothing new. I write this to instruct regarding mail. We have a U.S. post-office department here now.[66] You can send mail matter to me same as in U.S.

Address: Cavite, Philippine Islands
Station #1 Lieut. Geo F. Telfer, Co. L 2nd Regt. Infty OR USV

Mail goes from here direct to San F. today. Next mail out will be via Hong Kong — but rate of postage is the same (2¢).

Send the photographs I asked for.

We have not received mail yet — except the little that came on second expedition. The *Newport* is here but she did not bring mail. We are watching the inlet for the mail steamer — due today.

No news — except that a few troops have been placed in the outposts between the Insurgents and Spaniards. There is talk that our regiment is to be left as garrison at Cavite — instead of being taken across to Manila. We don't like it, of course.

It is hot — always hot. We are all cross and disagreeable.

Much love to all.

Affectionately,
Have not been paid yet.   George

36

Cavite P.I.
Aug. 9, 1898

Dear Daughter Grace,

I was on guard yesterday and after a very trying day I came into the guard room very much out of sorts. And was most agreeably surprized at receiving your letter of June 30th and Mama's of July 5. I had about given up hope of ever hearing from you again. Everybody has had letters but me — on mail steamers. Your letters came via Vancouver and Hong Kong.

We expect an attack on Manila tomorrow. Dewey waited for soldiers, then more soldiers, then for the *Monterey*. The *Monterey* and 10,000 soldiers are here, but have had to wait for lighters to get them ashore.[67] Then the wind blew off shore and delayed landing — Now they are landed, and the *Monterey* has taken coal. The telegraph line is put up. The "neutrals" have moved their ships out of the way — and nobody knows why we don't act. Our men are getting sick — 80 cases of typhoid now, and officers are desperate at the inaction. The 2nd Oregon is to take no active part. At least we are not moved to the Manila side. We guard the supply depot and hospitals.

The view from the top of the wall of the fort is fine. First are the small river steamers loaded with refugees from the Pasig river, then our transports and supply ships. Then the foreign ships — except German — then our Navy — then the English ships of war — then a narrow stretch of water — then Manila — glittering white in the sunlight — waiting certain destruction if she does not surrender. Our war ships will move out to attack and the English ships will come in to protect neutrals. The officers of the 2nd Oregon will put on white duck clothes and take seats on the wall, and watch the fight 8 miles off.

Get the *Review of Reviews* for *June*. It has two articles on the subject of the Philippines which express the condition of the people and the country very well. Also, *Scribner's* for July. I want you to read all of them as it saves my writing long letters. The pictures are quite well selected and will give a good idea of the country.

We have the *Oregonian* to July 5. They send us a supply of each issue. So we are very well posted as to affairs at home.

I have just got settled in my quarters and now comes orders to move into another building tomorrow. The soldier's life is not a happy one.

We were all paid for May and June yesterday — and the men feel much brighter in consequence.

Your affect. father,
Geo. F. Telfer.

«15»

Manila P.I.
Aug 16 1898
Address as before only change to Manila P.I.

Dear Family,

We are in Manila. *We* — being the "household troops" did not fight.[68] Our regiment furnished one company — Case's as body guard for Gen'l Merritt and the balance with exception of Co.s C, M and I were placed on a steamboat and followed his (Gen'l Merritt's) headquarter boat throughout the fight.[69] As soon as the flag of truce boat came back with acceptance of terms of surrender, we were ordered ashore on the water front and Col. Summers was given charge of the Walled City[70] and charged with the duty of receiving surrendered property and maintaining order.

The account of the action will be stale reading by the time you receive this. It was a tame affair. I saw nearly every shot fired from the fleet. We were just out of range of fire, to one side, so we could see the flash of each gun and watch for the striking of each shot. The land force was advancing at right angles to the line of the fleet. They were on our right. The woods shut off our view of the troops but we could see the smoke and one brigade whose left was on the beach.

Our boat ran aground getting us to shore and we were landed in small boats. In consequence it was nearly dark when Co.'s H and L marched into the city from the Sea Wall. We were quartered for the night in the Administration building — or City Hall — Col. Summers not daring to seperate us in regular barracks. We had no baggage and no food except what we put in our haversacks in the morning. Stores were all closed, and there was nothing in the way of eatables to buy if they had been open. I had my rubber coat, which I spread on the hard floor for a bed. That was Saturday — this is Tuesday — I have not had my clothes off yet. I am dirty, sore, and tired. Have been sleeping most of the day and am in good spirits.

Sunday we moved into these barracks and expect to live here for at least three months. We have the stationery and office furniture of the "haughty dons" for our plebian use — but as the officers did not reside in barracks, we are hard up for sleeping convenience. Our bedding and other personal baggage is still over at Cavite. We are so accustomed to moving that we soon locate ourselves. And the excitement and danger of battle and living in a hostile city does not put us out any. But I did not get a chance to settle. Sunday morning I was ordered to take 50 men and cooperate with the city police in guarding the gates, there being fear that the Insurgents were about to come inside and loot the city. There are

38

seven gates and my command was distributed accordingly. Fortunately we have plenty of horses. I tired out 3 during the 24 hours following. I rode from gate to gate constantly. At the principal gate it was very exciting. The gateway is wide enough for a single vehicle to pass through. Beyond is the New City — and the open country. The refugees were pouring into the city from the front — where they feared the insurgents, and the families of officers were moving back from the outer fortifications. Soldiers by squads and regiments were coming in to turn over their arms. Every armed man had to be stopped and his gun and ammunition taken from him. Carriages and packs had to be searched for cartridges. Insurgent spies had to be looked after and suspects taken in charge. The local police kept the stream of vehicles moving and prevented blockades. Everybody rides here so the press of carriages beat Morrison St. bridge on a holiday. At 3:30 in the morning all was quiet and I tied my horse, spread my rubber coat on the granite pavement and laid down and had one hour's sleep. That was all I had. I ate some prunes and crackers — that was all I had for food. I got off at noon yesterday. Had no bed to sleep on. Borrowed one at night. It turned cold and the bed was rattan. I had my blouse for a pillow and a thin cotton shirt on. My rubber coat was my only bedding — still I slept. Have been asleep most of the day.

The water works have not started up yet so we are very short of water. Washing is out of the question. I went to a barber shop and got shaved so as to get my face washed.

My feet have blistered from heat and wet. The blisters burst and make raw sores. It rained hard this morning and I was able to catch enough water to bathe them — using a pocket handkerchief for a towel.

Tomorrow I take a detail of men and guard the Treasury building for 24 hours. This is very pleasant duty as it is a nice building.

Saturday
Aug 20, 1898

This letter don't seem to finish very fast. When I have time I am tired and must sleep — so can't write. I was at the Treasury as stated. Guarded over a million in specie and a big lot of confiscated wine.

Was on the gates again last night. Have just woke up and learn that there is a mail going sometime so will close this and write another when I am in shape. Having lots of trouble over grub. Live on sardines and crackers.

We have heard of peace negotiations — but are going ahead with running the city. A Provost Marshall Gen'l has been appointed and the police department will be fixed at once — as well as the rest of the Govt.

Affectionately,
Geo F. Telfer

Manila P.I.
Aug 24, 1898

Dear Lottie,

Have a few moments before mail closes. Have been on guard all night and have not had time to bathe and am not in writing mood. Am well and standing the racket finely.

Rec'd letter from Grace dated July 13 and from Mother same time. Letters are all very welcome I can tell you.

The Minnesota regiment is now inside the wall and is dividing duty with us. I called on some of them night before last. Charley Reeve is just the same.[71] Glad to see you—you think. Makes his officers do all the hard work, etc.

Col. Summers swells with a Landau and liveried coachman. Wants to take regiment home at once and splurge in Portland. Officers object. Say if he wants to go home, he can resign. We have all asked to have regt. assigned to regular army. Want to stay.[72]

Business chances here great. Of course money will be needed—but every mail brings enquirys from people looking for investment. Would prefer Honolulu—but the place is too small for the number who will rush in.

The weather is improving. They say October is their perfect month.

Everything in leather molds. Clothes sour as soon as worn. Envelopes and stamps stick together like fun.

Brigadier-General Summers (From *On to Manila*)

Am running officers mess for 4 companies, China cook and Philopena helper—neither talk English. Write often. Love to all. Must close.

Affectionately,
George

A gateway through the Manila wall. (OHS neg. 77396)

« 17 »

Manila
Aug 25, 1898

Dear Lottie,

I rec'd your letter of July 19 last night. I am very sorry you have worried so much. And I have sent letters by every ship which sailed. There has been nothing to worry about so far as my well being. If there had been anything to care about you would have heard by cable. Being here is no different from being away anywhere else.

Went out to dinner last night at Cardwell's mess. Met some old friends — one Dr. Fitzgerald of Minneapolis, also Cabell who had just arrived.[73] He has been appointed Captain in Adjt Gen'l Department and is asst. Adjt. Gen'l of one of the brigades here.

Dr. Ellis is just getting up from an attack of Typhoid. Is not out yet.

The water works are going at last and as we have elegant bath accomodations for officers and men, we are happy. We do not have to worry over water for domestic purposes.

Our bath room is a large one — about 25x50 feet — high ceiling. The floor is tiled and there are 3 tubs or tanks in the center — about 12 feet square and 4 deep, with a seat running around near the bottom — all stone. The water is run through a faucet *2 inches* in diameter and the outlet is 4 inches. So you see a tub can be filled and emptied very quickly. After morning drill it is very nice to get such a bath. There is an overhead shower in the center. The men have a similar arrangement only their tanks are larger — so that

half a company can bath at one time. These barracks are modern and have the most convenient arrangement I ever saw. They cover about 4 city blocks and are enclosed with stone wall topped with an elegant iron fence. The Administrative Building (where the officers are lodged at present) is in front. We can walk on a cement walk under cover — to the quarters of any company. The buildings include everything as to stables for the horses. We are most bothered for kitchens. Cooking is done here on braziers or open fires. Ranges are hardly known. Our sheet iron stoves are giving out and we have not learned to cook any other way. The Mess that I am running uses a "Klondike".[74]

We entertained two visitors at dinner tonight. It was my first effort. Everybody says it was a success. There is one American lady here — wife of a correspondent. We are talking of having she and her husband to dinner Sunday — that is if we can get our conversation and table manners down to the gauge of polite society. The life we lead is not conducive to refinement.

August 26 — Evening.

It is as lovely a moonlight night as I ever witnessed. The windows of our room look down on the parade ground and the men happen to be in a happy mood. Consequently we hear a singing and a large amount of talk — the officers have mostly strolled off to the Luneta or Escalta.[75] Another transport sails Sunday and I will try and finish this letter in time to get it off.

Mike, Co. L's Mascot. (Author's collection)

Our dogs are doing well. They report in line at all roll calls — two paces in front. The men have added a number of monkeys to their collection of pets. They are fastened to trees around the parade.

I am very sorry that you are all so anxious at home. We become so accustomed to death and sickness that we give little consideration to either. We roam around among these Spaniards as though we had never been at war with them. The first night I was guarding the gates — I took an escort when making the rounds. But the next time I did not think of it. Of course my revolver was in my belt in easy reach. The people here are more afraid of our revolvers than at home.

Aug. 27, 1898

Can't think of much more of interest to you. It is hot and we sweat, bathe and put on fresh underclothes. The merchants run the price of everything up because we are Americans. We change our gold into Mexican or Spanish dollars — getting a little over two for one — that is for $5.00 gold we get $10.00 silver. But the price of everything is advanced in the same ratio. Clothing is some cheaper — and most of us will stock up on summer wear. Eatables are all canned. It is hard to tell a grocery from a drug store. Everybody wears white duck and rides in carriages. It cost 10¢ (Mexican) to ride anyplace for as many people as can be got into a carriage. Or you can hire a Landau and 2 horses — 60 cents an hour.

The streets are being cleaned up and there are a few less smells.

My picture shows up in *Harpers Weekly* of July 16 — upper left hand corner of page in church group.

It seems odd to eat everything — including butter, out of cans. The butter is like vasaline in consistancy. The Spaniards do not eat much solid food — in this climate at least. They eat canned knick-knacks.[76] Sardines for instance. What we know as staples are unknown. Meat markets or provision stores do not

43

exist. Meat is sold in the market as we see it in Chinatown. We have canned roast beef as a ration — and the people think it a great thing and pay $1.00 a can for it.

There is a splendid opening here for the sale of American canned goods. They have been excluded heretofore — but are very much superior to the Spanish productions.

Now I will close this piece of patchwork. Stop worrying. This week will likely decide whether we return at once or not. You will doubtless hear as soon as we do.

Affectionately,
George

"My picture shows up in *Harper's.* . ." (From *Harper's,* July 16, 1898).

44

« 18 »

Manila
Sep. 1, 1898

Dear Grace,

Your welcome letter of July 23 was received yesterday. It is very good of you to remember your far off "paternal relative". I sometimes think I am almost forgotten. When one has lots of idle time on hand, and when surroundings are unpleasant, and the future is filled with suggestions of discomfort — at such times we grow homesick — or heartsick — or if among our younger officers — love sick. My idea is that the symptoms are the same. One of the symptoms is a tendency to feel aggrieved at acts — real or imaginary — of our friends. To consider ourselves slighted, etc. So I feel that I am not remembered according to my deserts.

We have been drilling on Dress Parades and reviews of late. This is the principal occupation of the soldier in times of peace. We are issuing white uniforms to the men and purchasing new uniforms for ourselves. This all preceeds parades and reviews in public presently. There are hints of dinners and balls for the future. We also dress up and promenade the Esculto during shopping hours and lounge or drive on the Luneta during evening display. From wrangling over tactics, military science, and outpost duty — we decend to discussing shoes, trousers, and shoulder straps. Our expenditures for toilet articles makes the store keeper's heart warm within him.

We get some amusement and are also anoyed at items floating through the home newspapers concerning Capts. Heath, Prescott, Wells, and myself.[77] The newspaper correspondents wanted news, we wanted action, and the general wanted information. We were *not* placed in arrest — nor was a court martial talked of. We had a nice trip and learned the country — gave the general information — and he expressed himself satisfied with the result of our expedition. We did not look for quite so much newspaper notoriety, however.

General Merritt has started for Paris — to attend the meeting of the peace commission. Before leaving he published a very complimentary order praising the splendid work of the second Oregon during the first 48 hours of occupancy of Manila — when they were alone within the walls — with millions of money and *billions* of property in their charge. As I had the sole command of the detachment of troops and "Civil Garde" which was detailed to take charge of the gates and regulated traffic in and out for 24 hours — the most trying of the 48 — I naturally take a great deal of the order to myself.

The dogs continue well. Tip has resented the presence of a native dog on our parade ground — during drills. They have broken up our formation several times by coming to words in our path. Today at drill I decided to let them settle the matter for good and all. So when they commenced I brought the company in to line at a rest and watched the fight for 5 minutes — at the expiration of which time our dog drove the other from the field amid our cheers.

Escalta Street Binondo, Manila. (OHS neg. 77386)

I expect to send this on a transport which returns in the morning, so will close. Am going to try and get some photographs of our surroundings and will try and write some descriptions. I have collected a few choice weapons to hang on our walls.

I have been looking for your photographs. I wrote that I did not have them in my case.

Tell Mama that a brother-in-law of Mr. Newhall — Lieut. Gritzmacher of Co. H rooms with me.

He is a very good boy and furnishes me all the amusement I have.

Pratt looks healthy. I see him daily — but have not had much chance to talk to him. Will do so however.

Am very glad you are having a jolly time. Be thankful that you do not live here or in any other Spanish country.

Love to all. Tell Willis I will answer his letter. I sent him a jacket — the kind worn by the musicians

46

Cart drawn by water buffalo. (OHS neg. *77499*)

in the Spanish army. It was my share of the "loot" in our company quarters. Tell Hazel I am sorry I could not hold her in my arms when she was hurt.

Your affectionate father,
Geo F. Telfer

« 19 »

Manila
Sep. 8, 1898

Dear Willis,

This is a funny country to our American eyes. To be on the streets — or to travel on a country road is more like looking at a picture book than anything else. Heavy teaming is done by use of two wheel carts drawn by water buffalo driven by a chinaman. The carts run without greasing the wheels and make a great deal of noise. You have seen pictures of water buffalo. They are odd looking beasts. They put a ring in their noses & drive with a rope hitched to the ring. The driver goes in front and pulls his buffalo around until he heads right — then goes back to his seat on the cart. When he wants to change direction he gets down & goes in front again. The chinamen are not like the ones we have in America. They are large, muscular men. They wear a pair of blue trousers which come almost to the knee. Their hats are the big bamboo affairs that you see in America. They wear nothing but the hat and trousers.

For carriage use, ponies are used. They are very cute. Some of them are very handsome and showy. The carriages are Landaus — high seat for driver — & a top over back seat. The wheels are small — like phaetons. The swells have coachman & footman dressed in white duck & top hats. Everybody rides. Officials have their own rigs. We have lots of them but not enough to go around. It is very nice to drive in the evening when it is cool & the breeze blows in from the bay. We pay $1.50 Spanish (75¢ American) for 2 hours. There is a one-horse covered cart that we use for shopping, etc. We pay 40¢ Spanish for one hour — 20¢ for each subsequent hour. Or 10¢ for a single destination. When I go out to buy for the mess, I dress in white duck, put on a money belt — with pouch in front. The money used is all silver & nothing smaller than 20¢ piece (in silver). The small coins are copper — 1 cent. So you see a great weight has to be carried. Nothing is delivered. I bring my purchases home with me — or hire chinamen to pack in on shoulder.

You know these islands were inhabited by Malays. The Chinese & Spaniards came about the same time. The Spaniards were so indolent that they allowed the Chinese to get a monopoly of trade. Then they became jealous & killed a few thousand of them. But the Chinese held on. The Spaniards have the "high-tone" trade & swell stores. But most of them are officials — priests or soldiers. There are four distinct races. The Malay, the Spaniard, the Philipeno (mixture of Chinese & Malay) and a light colored race — a mixture of Spanish and Malay.

We find that it is best to dress & live like the Spanish. If we exert ourselves in the heat of the day we are apt to be sick. So we get up early. Drill for an hour, lounge in quarters with very little clothing on until 5, when we have parade. After that we go over town & see the crowd. Business houses close from 12 to 3 — and close for the night at 8. At 6 the ladies & children go out in carriages & drive until 8 — when they go home for dinner. The men sit around the cafes & drink wine, smoke cigaretts & tell how they

"Securely guarded. 'B' on Duty." (OHS neg. 77394)

might have kept us out of the city. They drink wine in very small quantities & intoxication is unknown. I am sorry to say that the American soldiers disgrace themselves in this regard. We get along nicely with the Spaniards. They are very polite & until they see fit to blow us up with underground mines or dynamite — we will be on good terms. I am certain there will be trouble before the end. But — "sufficient for the day is the evil there of."

The monkeys would amuse you as much as anything. We have a lot of tame ones around our barracks. They live in the trees on edge of parade ground. They are one thing the dogs are afraid of. They will follow a dog all over & guy him. The dogs get awful mad but don't dare touch the monk. They — the monkeys — all know mess call & come down to eat. Every little while we hear a racket in a tree & down will come a string of monkeys & chase each other across the parade. They like to come up behind a man & run up his back & make him jump.

Sep. 9, 1898

I find that there is a mail going this morning so will close this. Have been under the weather on account of eating blackberry jam pie. Am feeling alright now.

There is still talk of our going home. But I dont think it at all likely before the first of the year. A lot of the sick are to be sent home this week. Some officers have asked leave of absence — but it has not been granted so far.

We have very little rain & the nights are delightful.

I suppose that you are in school again. I hope you will bear in mind that letter writing is a part of your education, and will make some effort to improve in that line. You *must* write oftener. Will have to close.

Love to all.
Your affectionate father,
Geo. F. Telfer

20

Manila P. I.
Sep. 11, 1898

Dear Lottie,

This letter will go per Str. *Newport* and she is expected to make the trip to San F. in 15 days — so you will have this in living time.[78] We don't know why the *Newport* is being rushed — but presume events are under way which will develop later. We are much worked up over peace negotiations and proposed giving up of this territory which we have taken. Naturally we would have pride in knowing that our flag would not be hauled down.

A gentleman by the name of Boeringer goes back by this same ship.[79] He is a celebrated artist and newspaper correspondent. He came out with our regiment and has stayed with us since our landing, and calls himself one of us. He has collected material for an illustrated lecture, and will proceed to Portland to arrange for delivering a series. We gave him a letter to Mrs. Jones and will urge him to call at the rooms of the Emergency Corps.[80] We hope our wives will meet him for he knows us each by name and can tell just the condition of each. Capt. Wells has written a letter to Mrs. Jones regarding need of nurses, etc. Urge this matter all you can. The lack of nurses and hospital supplys is the greatest scandal of the war. Think of a man sick with typhoid fever — with no nurse. Think of *50 fever* patients in one room with *one* man to look after them — that man a soldier, knowing nothing about the care of the sick. Take this room at night — without lights — except what is afforded by a single candle — carried by the attendant. Think of the misery of it all. Then add to this a lack of mosquito nets — to keep off flys by day and mosquitos at night — nothing but the commonest food — none of the prepared foods ordinarily given the sick — even a lack of medicines.

Crowne had an attack of measels and went to the hospital.[81] Of course he had his own nurse and a room to himself — but he told me that he would lay in the open air and die before he would face the horrors of a night in such a place — that is the suffering of the men. He said to hear some poor fellow calling for something and you know how many things are wanted by the sick — calling and calling until exhausted. He said no man could listen without being sick himself. Some one wrote a poem (during the Crimean War, I think) and some of it runs in my head day and night — "there was a lack of woman's nursing, there was a derth of woman's tears."

We buried one of our company a week ago — 17 forlorn — unmarked graves — besides those in Catholic cemeteries. — Nearly all the 17 deaths the result of *no* care. We need nothing from the people at home — that is from the women. We have food, clothing, and are comfortable — until we are sick — then *God help us*. What we want is trained nurses. The government can furnish supplys if the women insist on it. Do not waste money and time on anything else. Take the matter up with Boeringer. He knows just how we are fixed and can give practical advice. Tell the condition to your doctors and let every woman talk it constantly. We feel that something must be done to arouse public sentiment. We don't want any hospital ship. We have plenty of buildings. The doctors do all they can — but a fever patient requires nursing more than medecine.

I was one of the few who did not get a letter night before last. But we all received *Oregonians* up to Aug. 1st — and San F. papers of Aug 4. So we know home news to that time at least. You know mail comes regular now via Hong Kong.

We are expecting trouble with the insurgents. Several collisions have taken place and Aguinaldo is concentrating his forces north of the city which looks as though he proposed holding some territory, if not Manila.

We were much amused at an editorial in the Oregonian which said 30,000 troops would not be enough to prevent rapine and destruction if Manila fell — the 2nd Oregon did the job alone. The people of Manila never knew there had been a change — except that the soldiers were large and wore blue uniforms. With 50 men of Co. L, *I* held all the gates for 24 hours. One of our corporals with 8 men stopped one body of 2,000 Spanish soldiers and held them for an hour until he received instructions as to the disposition. The local papers say it was one of the most remarkable cases on record. Understand that we are the police, as well as courts of justice and all that pertains to the conduct of a city government.

We have 20,000 Spanish soldiers to look after as well as the mixed populations of large city and our own soldiers off duty. So you can imagine it is no picnic.

We have received *Munsey's* for August.[82] It has some

Spanish soldiers. (OHS neg. 77440)

excellent views of places in Manila. As soon as we have another payday I will send you some photos — of the company as well as myself. Just now we are all broke. We expected to be paid on Sept. 1 — but the Paymaster has not reached us yet. This is one of the hardships encountered by the expedition — utter incompetency in staff administration.

Have not called on Charley Reeve yet. My clothes are too shabby to be seen in public. Have new ones — when I can get money to pay for them.

Have you taken notice of a Mrs. Prescott from La Grande — wife of Capt. Prescott?[83] He has always been a warm friend of mine and writes that she met you at the rooms of the Corps. She is a commonplace little woman — but very good and if you have a chance pay her a little attention.

I wish the children could see the strange things which this country contains. It would be a whole circus for them. But there is no country like our own for women and children. This will be a great missionary field. Think of a christian country that has nothing but Roman Catholics in it. The Inquisition did its work well here.

When men have a chance they develop new traits. The funniest officer in our regiment, the one who says more downright comical things is Phillips of Albany.[84] The most popular field officer is Yoran. McDonald is by far the best drill master — but the "out of town" captains make better showings than those from Portland.[85] The major that I claimed to be the best officer in the state is a ghastly failure and we are all sick of him. And so it goes.

Lieutenant-Colonel Yoran. (From *On to Manila*)

Everybody says I am getting fat. I must be weighed and find out;

Don't worry about me — as regards sickness. The doctors watch officers very close. It is a serious matter to have an officer laid up — as it confuses things; Besides Ellis and Whiting are with the regiment and Cardwell is Brigade surgeon — all three take a personal interest in me.[86]

Grace is very good to write such nice letters. I appreciate them. I am sorry Willis is so negligent. And Hazel is forgetting me. I write every mail, so don't think *I* neglect you.

Affectionately,
George

52

21

Manila P. I.
Sep. 19 1898

Dear Lottie,

I write this as a sort of report as to my condition. *I am well.* We have nothing of greater — or less — importance to relate except perhaps that we are having a series of evening thunder storms, which interfere with evening drives and promenades.

Two officers were taken to the hospital today with typhoid — Brazee and Huntley.[87] It makes us a little blue. We have asked to be allowed to secure private quarters outside the barracks — but the C. O. is making a grand stand play on standing for the rights of enlisted men — and making his officers uncomfortable.

Moore expects to return on the *Rio Janero*.[88] He has been messing with us lately and promises to make a good report of my condition. He took our pictures today noon. Call on him when you learn of his return.

At mess today we were talking to Moore about being homesick. We all agreed that we had some pretty bad spells — but on a whole it was more our wanting to see wives and children than a desire to return to America. We all feel that having come so far and stood so much we would be doing wrong if we returned without seeing more of the country. Until the outcome of the Paris meeting is known, we shall be prisoners and consequently can see but little. And then we all dread the voyage home in a transport —

Have not recovered from the horrors of the voyage out;

I hear that Reeve has been made Brig-Gen'l. — but have seen no confirmation.[89]

Have gained about 10 pounds since I was weighed at Camp McKinley. If our personal surroundings were pleasanter I think I would be fairly contented. But I cannot get used to living ten in a room. If I could master Spanish so as I could talk to people it would be less lonesome. But it is harder for me to acquire Spanish than for a chinaman to talk English.

Our amusement is going around to the stores. The Anglo Indian houses as well as the Chinese merchants have discovered that the American is a goody buyer — and they are getting in big stocks of goods. They display them to us and offer bargains. As you know, the average man does not shop *much*. Therefore he is ignorant as to home prices. We see something pretty — ask the price — it seems resonable and we buy; Capt. Pickens came in the other day with a dress pattern for which he had paid $1.50.[90] It was a pretty organdie (I guess that's it). He thought it very cheap. We found that it measured 10 yards and our dry goods men said it sold for 10¢ in America, so he paid 50¢ more than his wife could have bought it at home for. Our men are buying all manner of Chinese and Japanese curios — which can be bought at Andrew Kans for less money.[91] I have done no buying yet, but I enjoy looking at the things.

We were paid off Thursday — and the boys have been "blowing themselves for keeps." It seems odd — but those of us who expect to do anything in the way of Christmas presents will have to be making a move. That is — we must find and purchase the present — then watch for an opportunity to send home. Of course none of us can afford to pay freight, so we must wait until a transport is returning. If the captain is good natured — he allows us to load him up. We, of course, paying freight from San F. From now on we will have officers or men going home invalided — and we can send by them. One of Co. H men — *Gantenbein* expects to go this week and I have a chance to send by him.[92] Of course everybody wants to send — and it is too much to load one man up with all that is desired to send.

Moore has been working to go back ever since he came and has played sick. He is no use to the command — so we all stand in and induce the medical department to recommend his being sent home. That is the only way to go. Resignations or leaves of absence are not approved. So it is either be sick — or stay. We arranged to put the convalescent sick of our company on board one of the ships laying in the harbor. We pay their board and they are the same as passengers. The few days they have been out has made a wonderful improvement in their conditon. The doctors say that the fever is no worse here than any place else — but recovery is slower on account of the enervating climate and lack of food and nursing. I think that all of these conditons could be overcome by establishing convalesent hospitals on the islands at the mouth of the bay — or on ships. I hope nurses will reach us in time. I notice by the *Oregonian* that efforts are being made to send some from Portland.

We need women for the general good of the command. We are becoming perfect barbarians. One would think we were all from the frontier; Refined conversation and table manners — gentlemanly acts of all kinds are forgotten. It is curse, swear, drink, and gamble from morning until night. And at table — it turns my stomach to see men eat. We have reached the hardened stage which follows bad treatment, neglect, and disappointed hopes. We are made to feel that we are dogs — and will soon become little better. If there were some refined women here it would hold things down. Of course we do not meet the Spanish ladies. They all belong to the official class and the caste prejudice is very strong. They do not even associate with one another on account of differances in rank. Besides, Spanish ettiquette is peculiar. Men entertain among themselves — but not en family — and then — we are *the enemy*. The high caste Fillipinos are *Insurectos* and dare not come into Manila and we don't go to the towns where they are.

Well this letter has spun itself out after all — and I am afraid you will feel somewhat bored. But if you do — you will only feel as I do all the time;

I am so alarmingly well that I don't see any chance of getting sick leave. I guess you will have to enlist as a nurse and come out.

Give love to all. Kiss the babies.

Affectionately,
George

54

« 22 »

Manila P. I.
Sep. 23, 1898

Dear Grace,

I am on guard. It is night, very warm and I am trying *not* to notice mosquitos, prickly heat, red ants, little rivulets of perspiration running down my back, fidgets in my feet, and a dozen or more other small things which make life in the tropics interesting. Everybody quotes Kipling — "East of Suez where the best is equal to the worst." — We all try to recall things Kipling has written. We appreciate Kipling here. He is the only writer who gives facts regarding the soldier's life in this climate — and makes the description interesting.

The ants are the most remarkable insects you ever saw. All the tables, or cupboards where you are likely to place food — must stand on feet, the feet placed in cups of water. If you drop a particle of food — within five minutes a party of ants are rolling it off. Where they come from is a mystery. They swarm over every thing. They are nature's scavengers. In one night they will clear away a large part of the filth which lays on to the ground. They are to Manila what the dogs are to Constantinople.

One of my sources of amusement are the native children. They are like darkey babies — only smarter. They are very dark but have straight hair — that of the boys is cut short. They have the negro features and white teeth. They are musical and catch all our popular airs. It is very funny to see a lot of them — nothing on but a shirt coming a little below the waist and open in front — playing soldier and marching to the tune of "Marching through Georgia" — sung by themselves. When we pass them on the street they stand up and gravely salute with the hand — as they see our soldier do. Sometimes we see them scratching each others backs — like the monkeys.

I saw a man take his baby in bathing the other day (the men take most of the care of the children). He held the baby in his arms and walked out into the water up to his armpits. Then, holding the baby close, he would sink down until both their heads went under. The baby was not over a year old. When the dipping had been repeated four or five times, he brought the baby out and the mother wiped it dry and dressed it in clean white clothes. It never cried or made any fuss.

It is a very pretty sight out on the shore drives — or boulevards — in the evening. It is the only time ladies are seen — that is Spanish ladies. They come out in carriages. They get out of the carriage and join groups of friends and promenade on the foot way — 4 or 5 abreast. They never wear head covering day or night. We distinguish foreigners by their having on hats or bonnets. The Spanish ladies dress in the European style — only a year or two back. The Mestizo or half caste have a style of their own. I have some photographs showing the two styles which I will send.

E.W. Moore started home on the *Rio Janero* yesterday. I sent a sword and some souveniers for you. He

55

said he would go over and tell you how I was. But he may have several things to do so you had better look him up.

Have had to chase out and settle a dispute between a driver and a party of Spaniards. As we are police we have to receive all sorts of complaints. As the Spaniards have a way of smacking the heads of hackmen who decline to be satisfied with the fare tendered, we have some interesting times. Just after I had got rid of the carriage party, I discovered a drunken soldier having a row with a lot of Spaniards down a side street. I made a run down and brought him out. I hope the rest of the night will be quiet.

Sunday
Sept. 25, 1898

Have had a holiday today. Capt. Wells, Lt. Barber and myself accompanied by an English resident, took a carriage this forenoon and have been driving about the outskirts of the City all day.[93] We went over the ground on which fighting took place. Examined earthworks, forts, blockhouses, and other fortifications, on both sides. The Spaniards made very complete and elaborate preparations for defense. They also had the best of cannon and small arms — but they failed to avail themselves of the one or use the other.

I talked with a Spanish resident a few days ago — who had been educated in England. He said — "You Americans are of the Anglo Saxon race. You are of the coming race. You have whipped us at every point and within 15 years you will confront us in Spain. Nothing can stop you. *We* can't. It is destiny." A sad state of affairs. Or perhaps a happy one for the world.

The Spaniards seem just as well satisfied to have us govern here as to govern themselves. They seem to have no energy, no pride. I suppose the office holding class feel the loss of income however.

We don't do much but look pretty. The men wear white cotton suits and white helmets. They fix up for guard mount with standing collars, whitened belts and have their cartridges polished like silver. There is great strife over getting the H.Q. orderly. This you know is the man picked by the Adjutant as the neatest in appearance. Co. L had 10 out of 14 days running. The officers wear white cotton trousers — blue blouses, white caps with black band, gold cord, and coat of arms (same as on blue cap). We have blouses made of a thin serge-like ladies' dress goods — not lined. We have all had new collar ornaments and shoulder straps made and look like fashion plates. But we sleep 10 in a room and fight. 5 long months of living together is too much. No privacy — no cleanliness.

We are looking for mail every day. Two transports are due. I did not get a letter the last mail. Hope I will this one. Of course we get all the general news — because each one tells the news contained in his letters, and we get a batch of papers and magazines every mail.

Tell Hazel that I would like to have a letter from her. My letters are written for you all and if I tried to

56

Destruction of Fort Malate by Utah Battery. (OHS neg. 77399)

write to each of you I would have to write the same thing 4 times — which would be tiresome to me and uninteresting to you. Willis should also write. He may regret not doing so some day.

Martin Pratt asked me to send his regards. He is looking well and says he has not had a sick day since he left home.

Well, my candle has burned out, and it is time for taps. The mail closes early in the morning, so I will close. Much love to all, and hopes that life is very bright for my little family.

Your affectionate father
Geo. F. Telfer

57

Manila
Oct 2, 1898

Dear Lottie,

The *Arizona* arrived last week with a big lot of mail. Everybody was happy. Some officers received. 20 letters. Some as late as Sep 3rd. *I received* ONE — and that dated Aug 13. The envelope contained, in addition to your letter (which was none-the-less very welcome), photos of Willis and Hazel and about *ten sheets of blank paper*. Some of my friends suggested that you thought I could not get writing paper here. Of course I had no right to expect a large number of letters because I do not keep up an extensive correspondence — but I did look for one of later date than Aug 13. I don't know when we will get another mail. There seems to be a delay in getting letters via Hong Kong. I suggest that you address letters to Manila P.I. via Hong Kong.

I am sorry you are so bothered for money. I have not been able to send any home as we are in constant dread of being ordered to change station and do not care to be in the position we were in when we came over. If the officer in charge of the commissary had not been good natured and stretched his instructions and advanced our expense money we would have been bad off. As it was I sometimes went hungry at Cavite. That was before the stores were off the ship. At one time Wells and I arranged to sell our revolvers to insurgents in order to raise money to live on. After the stores were off — the Commissary sold us on credit and we were all right — except that we wanted bananas, etc. but could not buy them even at 2¢ each. I find that it takes money to clothe oneself for this climate. White trousers don't cost much — but you can't *get* along with less than 6 pair. We have them laundered at 6¢ per pair — but there is a pair a day. Then your underclothing sticks to you and tears when you take it off. This requires a large supply. I got a lot of captured underclothing — but the Spanish soldier is so small that *his clothes will not fit Willis* — and I burst the shirts out at one wearing.

We are in hopes of getting extra compensation for this service. We did get an order stating that all overs should be mileage for the trip (amounting to $320.00 each) and were quite jubilant for a time — but a cable came which changed it to officers detached. One thing we have for the future is two months leave of absence before mustering out. This means $250.00 — for pay goes on and if one gets immediate employment he is that much ahead. We are also to receive back pay from time we were ordered into service — about $65.00 for me.

Mrs. Reeve is here. She came out with the last expedition. I have not seen her. I may call sometime. You must know that there is a vast distance — in this service — between a General and a lieutenant. Our Captains even object to sitting at table with lieutenants. A captain orders his lieutenant about as we once would have ordered a non com. This is *not according* to ordinary custom — but it is according to things here.

The Red Cross nurses arrived on last expedition. But the old monkey who attends to the killing off of

Spanish-American War soldiers recuperating stateside at Presidio Hospital, San Francisco. (OHS neg. 77399)

our sick men told them that he had no use for them and that they should not have come.[94] So our men are dying at the rate of two a day as heretofore. I took a typhoid case to the hospital this morning and was glad to see that the ladies were there as visitors—if not as nurses. You have no idea how much more cheerful things looked. They could not be—called beautiful—but appeared as Angels in those dens. Their coming will bring about some reforms I think. By the way what in the name of wonder did you ladies intend those woolen night caps for? The thought of them makes one shudder. We *do* wear a

59

fever band because we dont dare leave it off — but we don't wear much else at night.[95] You don't seem to realize what a night in the tropics is like. We notice that you are expending money to send supplies to us. We don't know of any having been received.

I had quite a little adventure a few nights ago. Dunbar and myself were returning from downtown about 9 o'clock.[96] When near our quarters one of the guards informed us that a woman had been stabbed, in a neighboring house. I sent word to the surgeon and officer of the Day and went on with Dunbar to look after the woman. We found her in the passage way of the house, laying on the stone floor in a pool of blood. It was an awful sight. The dark passage — lighted by a single small lamp. The woman still alive and giving an occasional moaning cry. Her hair — she was a native — hanging loose and soaked with blood. Her white waist stained the color of her red skirt — and her bare breast showing a knife wound just above the heart. Blood had ceased to flow when we found her. I was at my wits ends as to what to do. A large church — filled with Spanish prisoners was across the way and 4 or 5 priests came over — but they looked at her with as much sympathy as they might look at a dog — and did nothing. I could do nothing until Ellis came. He was as helpless as I. He said she was beyond help. All we could do was to have our men place her on a stretcher and carry her to the nearest hospital to die. The Spaniards could not see why we did this. Why not let her die in the street? The Roman Catholic church may do a great deal in the way of charity — but it is brutal in a Catholic country. I had to *order* the hospital officials to open the doors before they would admit our bearer. The woman lived about 10 minutes after. They *did* place a black cloth over the head and breast, after death. An hour after, at the provo office, we learned the story. The woman — a Fillipena 18 years of age was standing talking to her husband, when a former lover came in and drove his knife — with the wonderful skill these people have — into her heart. Then disapeared. The husband called our sentries on duty at the church, then went back and stayed with the woman until sent to the provo. Such affairs are quite common here. Nevertheless it is sad — in our eyes. But we are becoming accustomed to death and blood letting in all forms. Our nerves are not disturbed at least.

One form of dissipation exists here — in worse degree than in America — the eating of peanuts. We have large baskets of them standing in every room — and we eat most of the time. Even I have now and then indulged — showing how low one may fall when separated from the refinements and restraints of Western civilization.[97]

The *Oregonian*s received are filled with accounts of, and comments on, the bad conduct of the Oregon regiment. (The whole of the *Sun* story is a *lie*).[98] We have chipped in $1.00 each today, to pay for a cable to the *Oregonian* stating that the charges are false. We do not mind these attacks as much as we do the failure of our friends to take up our fight at home.

The comments and interviews in the *Oregonian* sting I can tell you. Gen'l. Anderson is very indignant and has sent Col. Summers a personal letter saying so, also one for publication which goes by this

60

mail.[99] It would seem as if it would be needless to deny any stories of the kind published. That we were sent from home with incomplete equipment. That our State failed to supply the enlisted men with money, shoes, and shirts. That the food furnished by the war department was not adapted for use by men in the tropics. That the Medical department did not furnish medicines ordinarily required. All these things are known and will of course be corrected in time—(perhaps we will all be dead however). But that people at our own homes should side with people in the East—(known to be envious of the partiality shown us by Gen'l. Merritt, Anderson, and Otis) is the attempt to prevent the government from giving promotions to our officers.[100] The harm cannot be undone now. It is too late. The President has made his appointment and we—who are still holding responsible posts in Manila are—left out.

Capt. Moon writes you today regarding an attack made on him in the Eugene *Guard*.[101] As I told you before leaving Portland—the men in the ranks are always wanting money. They expected the $100.00 given was to be divided amongst them. Not realizing that $100.00 divided among 80 men does not go far. As advised by Col. Jackson, the captains are holding their fund for emergencies—and I can tell you we all see lots of places to use it in the near future.[102] We have no means of getting money for unusual purposes without long delay. For instance if a man dies, it sometimes is very difficult to get a coffin and hearse from the Quartermaster—that is, without delay. And a slight mistake in the form of requisition would throw the whole matter out. At first the Q.M. re-fused to furnish coffins on the ground that it was the custom of the country to put the body in the ground without one. Of course these are unusual cases—but *if* they do come up—what can the captains do without money. The captains all claim that they are accountable only to the Ladies of the Emergency Corps for this money and decline to put the money in the public funds—or render accounts to anybody else. This of course causes some feeling. In any case pay no attention to attacks made by irresponsible people.

Small pox has broken out which adds to our numerous troubles. Not to mention a large number of men attached to the "Asiatic Squadron"—a line of disease which you may perhaps surmise the nature of.

The officers expect to be moved to better quarters this week.

With much love to all.

Affectionately yours,
Geo. F. Telfer

61

« 24 »

Manila P. I.
Oct 3, 1898

Dear Lottie,

I am still on "sick report." Out of all the Lieutenants with the regiment only *7* are available for guard duty at present. In our room Kelly is the only one on duty.[103] Dunbar goes to the hospital today with typhoid symptoms. Barber has malaria like myself. We sit and blackguard each other all day. Sometimes I go two days with no fever at all. At first I supposed I was well. But experience teaches us that you don't get well that quick. The slightest exertion brings the fever on again. You can't go in the sun at all. There is nothing for it but lounge around quarters and keep cool. Gritzmacher is off in a tent by himself — Small pox suspect.[104]

Most of the time we are pretty jolly and inclined to make the best of a bad situation. But of course we get blue now and then.

The weather is very nice. Cool nights and days bright but not very hot. It is strange that the fever attacks us at a time when the weather makes it possible to go out.

The papers today say that the U. S. has demanded the Philippines and the Commission has adjourned. I imagine there will be something of a delay. The English people here of course are anxious to have us hold these islands as it insures their mercantile enterprises. They think that England will purchase them from us — or trade Jamaica and the West Indies to us for them.

The hospital ship *Scandia* has been condemned as unfit for the purpose and will be sent home.

Most of the regiments are arranging to run hospitals for their own sick. The Minnesotas and some others having plenty of money can do this in good shape and it is surprising that they have not done so before. I don't know how we are to do anything because we have no money.

The Red Cross ladies have a very nice little hospital over in Malate. It is a new dwelling house and very fresh and clean. It seems good to go into one place where women are at work. The forlorness is somewhat lessened. Everything is neat as a pin. They have native help — which is good if you can handle it. Man may be ever so kind hearted but things will look uncomfortable and dirty.

The men are arranging for a Thanksgiving dinner. Our company is trying to arrange theirs at the English hotel. I don't know just what the officers will do — if anything. We are so divided up that it is hard to come at anything like united action. This *rank* question causes much feeling and prevents friendly acts. When a captain makes a scene in a mess room because a lieutenant happens to be waited on before himself — you can imagine that the lieutenants do not enthuse over union dinners.

Dr. Ellis is thinking of having Bertha come out. Many of the married men are talking of having their wives come. Some of them are so situated that it would be economy to do so. If the U. S. holds the islands and designates certain "posts"—of course quarters would be provided—or money allowances made for same. As it is now we are in the field—and officers will have to rent their own family quarters. The average rent of small houses is $25.00 to $30.00 per month—Mex.—equal to $12.50 to $15.00 gold. The Steamship companies are making a half rate San F. to Hong Kong for officers wives.

One of the amusing things here is to see the sewing woman at work. The natives all squat—or sit on their heels as we see the Chinamen. A woman sewing sits the same way and sews with a *Singer Sewing Machine*. These machines are made for their use and do not have a treadle. They are raised about a foot from the floor and are worked with a crank on the right hand. The machine is geared up to high speed and it would surprise you to see how fast they run. The woman takes her machine with her when she goes to a new place. Some of them sit on low stools instead of their heels. The work is spread on the floor around them.

In native tailor shops all the work is done on the floor—no benches or chairs. In the tin shops it is the same way. Four or five workmen will be soldering and making pans and kettles—all squatted on their heels and their work on the floor—instead of on benches.

Flat irons are round—have a handle a foot long. The top of the iron is an iron pot in which a fire is built. They put a blanket on the floor, place the garment on it and then shove the iron over it.

We have a pay day coming soon and if I am not *too* sick I will send some money. I don't dare go broke if I am laid up, because I might want to go home or some place for change of air.

I wrote Willis that I was not at all pleased with his neglect of duty in not writing to me. He is getting too old to be acting in such a slipshod manner. He must brace up.

Tell Hazel that she has not remembered me as often as she used. She was such a good letter writer.

You must remember this narrow life makes us very fretful and we notice small slights more than ordinary. Letters are the only things we have to look forward to. So don't think it strange when I find fault.

Affectionately yours,
George

«25»

Manila P. I.
Oct 7, 1898

Dear Grace,

After several days of heartache a delayed mail blew in and brought me your (also the rest of the familys) letters — under date of Aug 20.

You can form no idea of how homesick one feels after a month of the kind of life we are leading, and then a mail ship with letters for everyone but yourself. We devil each other and put a cheerful face on life and think we are all right — until then — and *then* we collapse. The sensation would be hard to describe. However your letters are very comforting when they do come. I am very thankful that you know how to write letters — and think enough of me to give the time to their composition. One passage in your last I read aloud to "the room" — and the roar of the laughter which went up was worth hearing. It is where you speak of the goings on in court. You mention the usual divorce cases, petty theiving etc. and close by saying — "*but since you left there have been no cases worth mentioning.*" Now if you will read the passage with an accent on the word "*you*" you will catch the point of the joke. Taken in connection with the amount of chaff I have poked at me on account of my recent newspaper notoriety — you may understand that it amused the gang wonderfully.

I send by this mail two photos — intended to show two types common to Manila. The Mestiza — is mixture of Spanish and native — usually some Chinese blood as well. The picture shows the dress to perfection — but the face is not as beautiful as some. The Spanish woman has a large, sharp, pointed nose. The Mongolian in the Mestiza shows the flatter nose — making a perfect feature. The other picture shows the Fillipina or Tagal type — from which the Mestiza is bred. The Mestiza is very light skinned — but black hair and eyes. The men (Mestizo) are very handsome. The upper part of the ladies costume is made of the famous "pina cloth" — embroidered. There are two parts to this garment — the neck piece and the waist. These are always made one way — and a Mestiza never has it of any other material. Pina cloth is hand made — from pineapple fiber. It looks like "bolting" cloth — only the mesh is irregular. It is the same color. It is *never dyed*. Some have been fooled into buying foreign manufactured goods in pinks, blues, etc. and have sent them home for Pina. These Chinese merchants are full of such tricks. If Mama was here she could have lots of fun in the stores. We buy most of our "furnishing goods" from Chinese peddlers. Two of them will walk into our quarters — staggering under great bales of dry goods. They unpack in the middle of the room and proceed to invigle us into buying. We can't drive them out — or freeze them out, so we make the best of it and have some fun. They have dress patterns, shirts, table cloths, napkins, handkerchiefs, etc. etc. If we get the price down one half, sometimes we buy.

The jewelry stores of Manila are much finer than anything in Portland. It is claimed that one store is as fine as anything in the U.S. Other stores do not make displays and it is hard to judge of their extent.

A Manila store similar to those described in Letter 25. (OHS neg. 77389)

There are thousands of merchants here. Having stores of all sizes from 8x10 to regulation 20x50. There will be — for instance — an entire block of Dry Goods stores — 8 feet front and about 15 deep — counter across front and customer stands on sidewalk — like peanut stand. Then there will be a block of hardware stores — same size but no counter. You go inside and select goods from glass cases on wall. Then shoe stores, furniture stores, etc. All on same plans. A building appears to be owned or run by one company or firm. The salesmen work on percentage and each has his or her room. The same articles are found in each.

Col. Summers sends a letter to the *Oregonian* by this mail.[105] Wells wrote it and it is correct — not exagerated.

The mosquitos are biting my bare arms and I must get under my net. So good night.

Your affectionate father,
Geo. F. Telfer

« 26 »

Manila P. I.
Oct. 7, 1898

Dear Willis

I was very glad to receive a letter from you a few days ago — under date of Aug 21. It seems a long time between letters.

You are wrong about the Manila fight. The Oregons were the only troops in Manila. The California & other troops captured Malate — a suburb like Albina is to Portland. The trenches were out there & the only conflict was out there. The city of Manila was entered by a part of the Oregon troops as soon as the guns from the fleet had silenced the batteries. It was expected that we would have a street fight — if not at the waterfront — where we had to land small boats. But the Spaniards had no fight in them — and *we* think would have surrendered without a shot if they had been allowed. We acted under Gen'l Merrit's orders — direct — and were near him all day. When the flag of truce was displayed — he ordered Col. Summers to enter the city with him. Co. F (Capt Case) acting as his body guard. As soon as the articles were signed — Col. Summers was ordered — by Gen'l Merritt — to detail one company & take down the Spanish flag & hoist an American flag which he sent for the purpose. Co. A — (Capt Heath) was detailed. An officer from the navy & Lt. Povey of our Company — hauled the Spanish flag down & hoisted the American. Co. A presented arms. Our band played the "Star Spangled Banner."

Col. Summers was entrusted with the duty of attending to the carrying out of the Articles of Capitulation. Every Spaniard who was disarmed by our regiment & every piece of equipment was cared for by us. The other troops did not enter the city for 10 days after. The stories about flag raising, etc., as told in papers we have seen, refer to affairs out at the trenches. At the present time the 13th Minnesota, 23rd Regulars, and 2nd Oregon constitute the Provost Guard of the City of Manila. The Minnesotas patrol the streets and are the same as police. The 23rd and the Oregon guard Military Stores and look after public buildings, etc. The other troops are quartered in the outskirts — that is — the part of the city outside the wall. They do patrol & outpost duty. Three companies — C, M, and I — stayed at Cavite under command of Maj. Eastwick. They took no part & did not come here for a week after we came.

We were treated with so much consideration. Had the finest quarters, were provided with new uniforms, etc. — that the others became jealous and this resulted in getting the newspaper correspondents to misrepresent us in every way. This is hard — but can't be helped.

The only amusement our men have is the Circus. A Filipino Co. give a performance in one of the theaters nightly. They do not have any horses — it is mostly gymnastics after the style of the Japanese troops we see at home. They have a ring in the middle of the theatre floor — instead of on the stage. I went one night. The performance was very good. Their clowns are very funny. They speak broken English & it would make a sick man laugh to hear them.

Horse and cart similar to those mentioned in Letter 26. (From *On to Manila*)

The performance closes with a pantomime. These people are natural born actors, as well as musicians. They also have a high sense of humor. So their pantomimes are worth seeing.

I blow all my spare change riding. Two of us usually go out in a Victoria after supper. We drive on the Luneta — or beach drive. The cool sea breeze after the intense heat of the day is all that keeps us alive. We usually stay out about 2 hours. This costs us 50¢ — (25¢ each). And if you could see *the style we put on*! Sentries all presenting arms, and soldiers —

Spanish & American standing at attention as we pass — I don't know how it will seem to ride in electric cars again.

Speaking of electric cars — reminds me that you speak of studying electricity. Keep it up. I dont know of anything I would rather you should give attention to. Write often.

Your affectionate father,
Geo. F. Telfer

67

«27»

Manila P. I.
Oct 8, 1898

Dear Lottie,

Mail closes at 11 o'clock and it is now 9 — but I will write a few lines in answer to your letter of Aug 21. I was very glad to receive this — for I felt rather sore at not receiving letters of a late date on the previous mail. I wrote Willis last night regarding our part in the capture of Manila. We had as much to do in the action as the others — but the city surrendered before we were landed. All troops in line of battle do not necessarily come under fire. If there *had* been as much resistance as one would naturally expect — with the splendid fortifications, etc. — We would have had a hot time. But the guns of the U. S. monitor, *Monterey* and *Monadnock* were in our line — trained on the city — and so great was their terror of bombardment, that the worst Spaniard among them did not even *scowl* at us when we marched up the street. Col. Summer's letter gives a very good — though brief — account of the work performed. The guard at the 7 gates mentioned was composed of men from Co. L and "Civil Guards" (police) under my command. This I wrote about before.

Of course we know nothing of events in our own country — so can form no idea as to what will be done with these islands. Naturally *we* think they should be retained.

I think the Volunteers will be replaced by regulars as soon as possible. I would try for an appointment in regular army but am too old. One having the "pull" might make it, but as a rule there is strong objection to appointing men over 25 years of age.

I am glad you had a chance to go to the theatre. You don't get enough amusement. I am also glad on Grace's account.

I think you were wise in getting the new teeth.

I wish you would send your picture.

I am moved. The captains and field officers were moved out of this building and the Lieutenants have 4 large rooms to themselves. I am in with Barber, Kelly, and Dunbar. Each has a corner. I have a bamboo screen to enclose my dressing room. A Spanish officer's field desk. A bamboo chair, floor, and bed mats and my cot. For the first time since leaving home we are living like Christians. I have what few knick knacks and photos I own displayed — and wish for more.

Don't send stomache bands.[106] We get a better kind here — captured with other military stores. They fit better than the American make. I got a lot of them.

Our rooms open up — like taking the front out of a doll house. We never close except for rain. We are on the second floor overlooking the street. There is a Spanish family across and we look into their rooms — one can form a good idea as to the manner of living. We amuse them as much as they amuse us, I suppose. Everybody makes his or her toilet at the window. When you wash you empty the water into the street below. When I came to the room, Kelly had been occupying it for some time. I wished to change my trousers and closed the blinds. He wanted to

68

"A lot of them sell fruit on the curbstone opposite our gate." Letter 28. (OHS neg. 77397)

know why I did so. I said I did not care to change my clothes with a whole family looking on. He said that he couldn't see what differance it made as they never took the trouble to close their blinds when they dressed. This will give some idea of the customs. A woman is caged behind iron bars all the time — except when she drives out in a carriage. She cannot go any place with a man — other than her own family. But in the evening — on the Luneta — she can leave her carriage, and promenade bare headed — without escort — among a crowd of soldiers of all grades. Their customs are full of strange contradictions.

Well I must close. Knapp telegraphed his wife not to come — afraid of small pox.[107]

Affectionately,
George

69

《 28 》

Manila P. I.
Oct. 9, 1898

Dear Daughter Hazel,

I intended answering your letter by the last mail — but my "think tank" got empty and I had to put it off. All the same I was glad to receive a letter from my baby. I had begun to think you had forgotten me.

So you had a birthday? And I was not there to spank you, too bad. What lots of things you must have bought for 50¢. Over here there is not much for little girls to buy. Andrew Kans store has everything that can be bought here. For some unknown reason they do not even make candy. All the candy I have seen so far is brought from other countries and is quite expensive — and not very fresh. A few cheap dolls — not fit to live in the same house with Jane — are to be had. There is a poor kind of ice cream (made from condensed milk) — but no ice cream Soda. The white children don't seem to have much fun. They are dressed in very unbecoming clothes, and have but little to amuse themselves with. They stay in the house all day and try to keep cool. They look through the bars of their windows at us when we pass — and appear so forlorn that we stop and try to talk to them. As they don't understand English we don't make much headway. But we give them oranges and "pickininney money" (large copper pieces of money). They all like the Americanos on this account, and if we happen to meet them on the street they trail us with delight and grab hold of us — laughing and chattering as hard as they can. It is often very hard to get away from them. They have large black eyes and their skin is very white and they look sickly. We always say "Hello Pickininny!" or "Weno Muchae!" — (if boys) or Weno Mucher! if girls (*nice boy* — or *nice girl*) and shake hands with us. *Some of us* think of *our* children far away — and are glad to see these little ones. The first morning in Manila four of us were out trying to find a breakfast. We passed the window of a small Orphanage — and the children swarmed to the windows — to see the "Americano Officials." It had been *two months* since we had seen a white child. We stayed there nearly an hour, and gave them all the spare change we had.

The native children have lots of fun. They are like the darkeys down south — and can make fun out of anything. They stay out doors all day — and play all the time. The older ones carry the smaller — but play just the same. The girls dress just like their mothers — in long red skirts, white waists, with one shoulder bare. Hair in a pug.[108] Toe slippers with wooden soles (or barefoot). When they run the slippers go "flip flap" — make a great racket on the pavement. They all have even white teeth — which they show a great deal.

A lot of them sell fruit on the curbstone opposite our gate. I have lots of amusement watching them from the window. They sit on the curb — put the tray of fruit in the gutter — and when the ground gets hot for their feet — they put them on the oranges to cool. We peel the oranges before eating.

Hazel Telfer. (Author's collection)

Now I shall expect a nice long letter from you by next mail.

Your affectionate father,
Geo. F. Telfer

Manila P. I.
Oct 15, 1898

Dear Mother,

Your very welcome letter of Aug 21 was received by last mail. It is a hard proposition to read a letter a month old and then write an answer to be read a month and a half after and have the original subject made clear to the first writer.

I write to Mrs. Clarke by this same mail. I promised her that I would. But there is so little to write about — compared with what people imagine there should be. We are supposed to be heroic — when we are not. War is terrible commonplace when you are participating.

The only real interesting subjects we have are the magazines and newspaper articles written about us and the country we are holding. It is astonishing how little truth there is written.

Then men who did so much talking about what they were willing to do — and fought so hard for appointments and worried over chances of not passing examination — are now making everybody miserable — because they want to go home. They act like a lot of girls who go from home for the first time. The average soldier is bad enough — but the officers are worse. Inaction is very trying. We older ones knew that war did not mean constant fighting. That armies frequently lay idle for a year at a time. So we were prepared to face this trying period. But the younger

Mrs. Emmeline Telfer, George's mother.
(Author's collection)

our government does not think it necessary for its soldiers to know the late news. So until we receive the *Oregonian* we are in ignorance. The *Oregonian* is very good and sends us a good supply of every issue. So do the San F. papers.

The Medical department is the only real exasperating thing we have to contend with. The medical officers as a rule are bright young fellows and try to do what is right — but the chief is a weak old gentleman — way behind the times. And then there is a fearful lack of necessary medicines. We suffer for the want of disinfectants — although a special appropriation of $75,000 was made for their purchase — for this expedition.

The Red Cross ladies arrived — but have not been allowed to work in the hospitals. They have a hospital of their own — but we can not send our men there — so it is of service for officers only. But the ladies come to the barracks and cheer up our men who are sick there — and make us all feel brighter.

The Monsoons have shifted and we are having a season of hard rains and cool weather.

The Military Board of health is having the City well cleaned and the rain is helping them. So we don't have that choice assortment of indescribable smells that we did.

I am glad "the family" recognize the fact that I live.

Write when you feel like it. Letters are always acceptable.

ones expected to land under a heavy fire — and fight their way to glory in a few weeks. I did my best to explain the probable line of action on the way over — but they would not believe me. Now they are aggrieved.

Of course you know more about the prospects of holding the Islands than we. And you will know the result of the Paris Commission before we do. There is a cable here — but it costs money to telegraph and

Affectionately yours,
Geo. F. Telfer

« 30 »

Manila P. I.
Oct 16, 1898

Dear Lottie,

A rainy Sunday in Manila is the same as a rainy Sunday at home. Sleepy. We are having a season of hard rains now — and so do little outside work. I had one of my bad headaches last night and am somewhat knocked out today. I took some compound cathartic pills and they make my stomach feel badly.

While I think of it — please send me a bottle of your "fathers medicine." I am troubled with constipation and fruit doesn't seem to help me as one would suppose.

The next time any of you see Mrs. Swinton ask about Mrs. Barber.[109] She is a neighbor of theirs and Dr. Barber is one of my roommates and usual companion in rambles about Manila. He is a very bright man and has traveled a great deal.

I don't see much of Capt. Wells. He is quartered in a building outside the barracks, and only comes over for drill, etc.

I stand at our window evenings and watch the Spanish lady opposite put her children to bed. And the family adjust themselves for the evening. "One touch of nature makes all the world kin". So the Spanish mother with her children seems a part of my own life. Spanish children and Spanish mothers are the same as American children and American mothers. There is the same skylarking as they undress, the same kiss and patting at bed time. It is the only glimpse I have had of civilization for many a long dreary month. I think that my nightly contemplation does me good. One becomes hardened by this life and something is needed to soften our natures. The family over the way is that of a Spanish captain, who was wounded twice during the war. He looks like Jno. Beeson.[110] His wife is a large woman — with a refined motherly face. There is a young woman about Grace's size — and age perhaps. She may be a daughter or a sister. I can't tell. There are two children about 6 and 8 years of age. It takes four people to wait on them. And they seem to live in two rooms. There is a man, a striker I suppose, who acts as a butler, etc. Two Fillipina boys who wait on table and look after the children — and a woman who sits on the floor and sews all day. The Captain comes to his window and looks out and we go to ours. The street is so narrow that we could easily converse across. If I understood Spanish I would cultivate their acquaintance.

I saw Mrs. Reeve the other day. She was sitting at a window. She did not see me, and I did not stop. She looks the same as ever. I cannot see that she has changed a little bit. I meet him once in a while. They have not found anybody who is going away and wants someone to live in their house. So they — the Reeves — are not living in any definite place.

Our sick — that is Co. L — are improving and we feel encouraged. Capt. Wells gives personal attention to men in hospital (I am sorry to say that most of the captains do *not*) and in his absence, of course, I do. I also look after men sick in quarters. The Medical officers fear an investigation and take great pains to carry out suggestions — as well as to show zeal in care of patients.

At my suggestion Capt. Moon made a protest in writing — or rather complaint — regarding a case of bad treatment in hospital. One of his men was sent to hospital — suffering with dysentery. He went to see him and found him in a tent outside the ward. It was a white tent — without a fly, and the heat nearly overpowered the Captain while there. The surgeon in charge assured him that the condition of the patient was in no way alarming. Seven hours after — the man was dead. Now white tents for hospital use are forbidden. Tents without flys are not tenable in hot weather. Dysentery patients must not be subjected to heat. So you see Moon had cause for complaint. His complaint was forwarded and reached Gen'l Otis — who sent for him and asked him to withdraw his complaint as it would make trouble. So it was withdrawn — but I think the Surgeon Gen'l had an unplesant half hour with the Military Governor.

I acted as Adjutant one week ago Sunday. Crowne was out of town. I had nothing to do but mount the guard. I got through it all right.

《31》

Oct. 18, 1898
Monday Night

On guard and sleepy. Have been on the jump all day. In addition to guarding stores, cannon, etc. we have a certain district to police. As we are making an effort to compel people to be clean, we have our hands full. Take a walk through Chinatown — then imagine 50 blocks like it — only every other place a liquor dive with unlimited back exits. Then put "high-toned" white people on the second floors. Have the second stories project over the street. Have the family horses in back rooms on first floor and the carriage in the hallway. Have the people educated to empty chamber slops, etc. — from windows onto the street below. Then think of the proposition in "Old Manila." Think of all the bad smells you ever ran against — combine them (in your mind) and you may have some idea of a Spanish city. We have a large street cleaning department and every foot of street is swept daily. Twice a day carts gather garbage from dwellings. This with disinfectants is lessening the smells a little. And evening work as police official is quite lively to say the least. At 7 o'clock I went upstairs to lay down a while. In about ten minutes a messenger came up to tell me that the patrol reported a crazy woman in the street near by. I sent men down to look after things — got Dr. Barber and went down. Found a Filipina woman in delirium (fever or small-pox — don't know which). She had been found laying in the street — where she had doubtless been put by the people in the house where she lived. Had to get an order to admit her to public hospital, get stretcher and lot of men to hold her and send her to hospital. Then send all the men to change their clothing and take baths in solution of carbolic acid — to prevent contagion. Went up stairs to get drink of water. Messenger came to tell me patrol had brought in some prisoners. Went down to office and found that men at outpost — hearing disturbance in one of the Spanish hospitals — had gone to investigate and found Spanish officer and men tying up a Filipina — who they said had stolen a truck. (They would have either killed him or cut off his ears or nose — they are liable to do either). Sent the batch to police station. The next patrol in, reported that Spanish lady had called them into her house to protect her family from servant who had drawn knife on them — and so it goes. Incidently, we hunt our men out of drinking dives. The Spaniards get them full and take their valuables from them. Two discharged regulars have been found floating in the river this week with bullet holes in their heads.

Please send me a small silk American flag — Pocket handkerchief size. One appreciates the flag of their country in places like this. These small flags we carry in our pockets and tie on canes when we want to demonstrait. If the Emergency Corps would send one to each officer it would be appreciated. A few have them. It is quite impressive — when the band plays "The Star Spangled Banner" at evening parade — to see the hats come off. All soldiers not under arms uncover, and all Americans do the same. The foreign residents follow suit — especially the Eng-

lish. All bands play this piece at retreat. All troops stand at attention and guards present arms. You have no idea of the solemnity on this occasion. The perfect silence — the sweetness of the music — all combine to add to the effect. The natives understand it to be in the nature of a form of worship — and look on reverently. The Spaniards do not dare show any disrespect. So it seems as if the whole city was at prayer. And we each ask — "How many of us will ever see the '*land of the free and the home of the brave*' again?"

Mail goes tomorrow via Hong Kong and I will send this. Hope I shall receive some mail myself soon.

Tuesday morning

A regular Portland fog hung over the city this morning — made us homesick. The sun is just breaking through and it will be hot. Nothing exciting happened after midnight and I went to sleep.

Will close in order to get this into mail.

Love to all,
Affectionately,
George

«32»

Manila
Oct 22, 1898

Dear Lottie,

Your letter of Sep. 4 was rec'd the same day I mailed my last letter to you. Also a stomach band and Grace's picture. Many thanks for the band. The picture looks down upon me as I write, and causes me to feel very thankful that I have such a sweet daughter.

A cablegram from Mrs. Knapp yesterday conveys the information that several ladies are coming over — "We know not when nor how".[111] I wish you could come. It is a selfish wish I know — for you would be very uncomfortable here. You are not built for a bohemian. I think it would be a grand thing for Grace. She would be so delighted with the strangeness of everything that she would not mind having the chickens for todays dinner tied by the leg to a chair in the sitting room, or having the horses in a room on the ground floor.

The weather is at its best now, and very fine. Of course it is hot during the day but very comfortable at night. It is the spring season — gardening etc. is under way. A large force of men are digging and cleaning the drives, walks, and shrubbery around the boulevards. In the country the truck gardeners are planting — and we have promise of lots of green vegetables. We have radishes and onions now. I eat onions, peanuts, and shave myself — thus have the mighty fallen.

I am sorry you are skimped for money. But all I can say at this stage of the game is — *don't worry*. It will all come out right in the end. I know that this is not very consoling — but I have been in such desperate straits during the last few months, that I consider that if one is alive — they cannot ask much more.

This paper is some that the Chaplain got to supply the men. My pens run through it fearfully. When we were all reading letters the other day — Barber threw his down and said — "Say! you fellows are full of resources, will you tell me how in h—l I am to take a parrot home?" — His wife had written him to bring one.

Kelly gets mail from half the women in Oregon. He is buying presents for the same number, I think. He spent $60.00 for handkerchiefs in one day.

Nothing new to write so will close.

Love to all,
Affectionately,
George

« 33 »

Manila P.I.
Oct 25, 1898

Dear Grace,

I am laid up — sick in quarters. Malarial fever —
that democratic disease which hits rich and poor —
high and low, with equal impartiality, couldn't let me
alone any longer. Everybody was surprised when I
gave up — as everybody thought I was fever proof. I
was taken Sunday. Fever ran pretty high for 36
hours and then went down. I am up and around —
but do not go out of doors. Of course I can't tell how
soon I may have a return — but hope it will leave
without further trouble. I have lots of attention. The
officers in my room see that I am cared for. And Dr.
Ellis comes up twice a day. The weather is bad —
cold and rainy. These house are not conducive to
comfort during a storm — as it is impossible to shut
them up. My cot gets so hard I can't stay in bed, so I
put on winter clothing and sit up.

I expect this letter will go on the *City of Paras* tomorrow. Lieut Huntley of Oregon City returns home
on sick leave, by same steamer. I did think it would
be nice to go — but his leave is for 30 days with permission to ask for 30 days more when he reaches San
F. He will just have time to get extension enough to
come back — if it happens that there is a transport
sailing at once. If there is *not*, he will have to make an
explanation to the Secretary of War. So it is hardly
worth bothering about.

Capt. Gadsby is trying to get away on the same

Grace M. (Telfer) Thorbus, 1902, twenty
years old. (Author's collection)

ship.[112] He is going home for good. His wife is an in-
valid and he has been trying to get back ever since
we came out. It is astonishing how many officers
there are here who did not want to come, but were
forced into it. When we were at Camp McKinley we
had an idea that everybody wanted *to come.*

77

When Gadsby gets back you must go and see him. He is an odd genious and a regular Englishman — but has been a good friend to me. Lt. Barber is in his company.

We appear to be having lots of trouble with the insurgents — that is I judge so after reading the home papers. *We* don't trouble ourselves much on that score. We think no more of the native troops than we would of a few companies of Chinese High Binders at home.[113] Of course they can cause trouble in many ways — but when told to move away from a position — they move. They stand in such mortal terror of our shooting — that they will never fight. Our fear is *fire* and cut water pipes, etc. We keep everything guarded and they do not get a chance to do much mischief. I hope things will be settled before many months.

Wednesday A.M.

The steamer sails this afternoon and I will get this letter off. Am feeling much better. Have had no fever for two days. So feel that I am about well — until the next attack.

The weather has cleared off lovely. You know how I like sunshine — so of course I feel better.

Capt. Gadsby has his leave and goes on the *Para*. He will resign when he gets back. If more sick captains would do the same, there would be a chance of promotion.

I send by this mail a copy of *The American* — our newspaper here — or one of them. In it is an ar-

Admiral Dewey, sketched from life on deck of the *Olympia*. (From *On to Manila*)

ticle translated from one of the Spanish (Manila) journals. We of course dare not take this view of recent events — as it will not do to belittle the achievements of our army. But if I were to write you a confidential history of the fall of Manila — I don't think it would differ *much* from the article in question. You people speak of Dewey's victory as the Battle of Manila. This is wrong. His was the battle of Cavite — or Manila Bay. The battle of Manila was on August 13, and fought by Meritt and Dewey combined. We call it an "Opera Bouff War." Some men were killed — *There was no need of killing anybody.* [114] The Spanish army code makes death the penalty for an officer who surrenders his post without a fight. So, you see there *had* to be a fight — but it was not where it was likely to damage property. No one knew what disorders might break out in the city — so Gen'l Merritt took the Oregon troops with him. *No other troops were allowed in the city for 48 hours.* When all was quiet and the Spanish troops disarmed — then one regiment of regulars and the 13th Minnesota were admitted. It will never be settled as to where the battle was fought — or who planted the first flags. The troops could not be restrained — outside — and they rushed pell-mell — firing as they went. Anybody who had a flag stuck it up on any building he came to. That was why the Oregon regiment was the only one allowed within the wall — the generals knew the others could not be controlled.

Well, my dear girl, I must close. I am glad you have made such a fine record for yourself during vacation. You are an ideal soldier's daughter. I wish you could come out and keep house for me here.

I send a small package of relics by Lt. Huntley who goes to Oregon City. He will mail them to you.

With love to all I am
Your affectionate father,
Geo. F. Telfer

«34»

Manila
Oct 29, 1898

Dear Mother,

I think I have not answered your last letter. I don't know that it makes much differance whether one letter from here is in answer to one from "*there*" or not. Events don't jibe enough.

I have recovered from my attack of fever. It was very light. Was not sick over two days. But as there is nothing to do I assumed that I was in danger of relapse, so stayed on sick report a week.

Our men are keeping in better health. We buy ice for the boiled water and so induce them to drink it instead of the hydrant water. We send armed patrols through the streets and drive them out of native houses and drinking places. We inspect their food, and investigate each case of sickness and generally find that the man eats too much. Five mornings in succession we line them up and give each man 5 grains of quinine. Then we stop five mornings and so on. In consequence the number of new patients is on the decrease; It is true that we get our fever cases back very slowly. This is because there is nothing to rally them. If they leave the hospital they will have to work. They would cheerfully fight, but work *is* irksome. All our care over these men, keeps them in reasonable health — but wont we catch it from the newspapers!

In most of the officer's messes the same food is

79

used as is issued the men (only the officer has to buy his). We find that good, appetizing dishes can be cooked — when our cooks learn how to season and prepare. The canned beef which the men *will not* eat — we find superior to the fresh beef issued here. We make it into stews, pies, and hash. There is a great deal of talk at home about how well the officers live and how poorly the men — But what we get from the men is paid for. Tomorrow, for dinner my mess will have ice cream. I *pay the company cook 20¢ cash for each dish*. The bread we use — I pay the company 10¢ per pound. This money they put in their own mess fund to buy delicacies. I have a man from the company to cook. I relieve him from all company work and pay him $10.00 a month, in addition to his government pay. I don't know how the eastern troops are treated — but this is a fair example of the way ours are. Of course the life of the soldier is hard — it cannot be otherwise. But it has always been so. As soon as he settles down to looking after the bettering of his own condition he will be more comfortable. Most of our companies are finding men who are skilled in cooking — and putting in a little money toward hiring them. In consequence food is improving. By the time they get home they will think home food very ordinary compared with that of the camp.

You will remember that I was one who sided with the President in delaying the commencement of war. Congress and the people had opposed the increase, in as well as the reorganizing of our army. Our staff-departments were poorly organized. And there were no supplys of — clothing, food or medicine. *You* think the President weak — and to blame for conditions. He was guilty of one fault. Alger.[115] Alger was a soldier. A popular hero. A man backed by the GAR and people who were supposed to know what constituted a good war secretary. If he did not appear to have the right stuff in him, who did? From start to finish there has not been a blunder in the field or on the sea. Never in history have such results been obtained in so short a time. In judging the President, give credit for the good.

It amuses us to read of the wails sent out by the Eastern troops over the crowded condition of transports, during that short voyage to Puerto Rico. *We were 36 days in crowded transports.*

I am glad to know that the family — east — still live in hopes of doing something with their gold mining scheme. It is well to live in hope.

They have *roses* here. Not very large nor rare ones, but just the same boys and girls peddle button hole boquets made of roses.

Grace's letters are a source of great comfort to me. She writes comforting letters. The kind that make you glad you received it.

It is very lonely here. Crowds of people — but none who can understand our language. And if they did — what under the sun could you talk about? Well I will consign this to an envelope and let it go for a letter. Much love to Auntie, and to your correspondents in the east.

Affectionately yours,
Geo. F. Telfer

80

«35»

Manila P.I.
Oct. 30, 1898

Dear Billie Boy.

I don't get as many letters from my boy as I could wish. I suppose you think you haven't much to write — and all that. But you must remember that we all have to learn to make up letters. You must learn to review the thoughts that have gone through your head, for a past week, and reduce them to writing. This is just as much a part of your education as the multiplication table or anything else. I want to know what you are thinking about just as much as I want to know what you are doing. You are getting on in years, and I must know what you are going to make of yourself.[116] I want to help you all I can, and you must give me some idea of your hopes and aims.

I sent you a map of Manila a while ago. It is quite correct. The city wall shows — but like everything else that is Spanish — it is not quite truthful. The wall is not double. The outer wall is an earthwork only. That is, it is stone with earth and grass covering it. The large Krupp guns are on these outer works. This is doubtless the finest specimen of a walled city in the world today. It is a grand piece of work and I never tire of looking at it. You can walk clear around the city, on top of the wall. In fact you can drive a team there. Of course this wall is not solid. It is a labyrinth of rooms, magazines, and dungeons below. All massive arches overhead — dripping slime and wet. The top is protected by a parapet and a great many canon are mounted there. These canon are useless, being old muzzle loaders and bear date as far back as 1700. These are the kind used in the War of the Revolution.

To go outside we pass under an archway with guard rooms on either side, and wide enough for a single conveyance. At the outer end of the archway are two heavy wooden gates. Outside of these is a drawbridge about 16 feet in length. These bridges are hinged at the inner end and hoist with a chain and windlass. The outer end of the bridge rests on a stone bridge across the moat. These stone bridges have a 4 foot parapet on either side. They are built on a curve. At the farther end the bridge enters another arch — passing through an outer fortification. This arch closes with gates and drawbridge the same as at the inner one. A hostile body in approaching the gate — comes over a road way and enters the outer gate in a line parallel to the wall — so would be subject to an enfalading fire.[117] When it gets through the outer arch it has to follow the curved bridge and cannot get into position to direct shots against the party guarding the inner gate. Of course these walls will not stand modern artillery. But they would be almost impregnable to infantry attack.

The fort at the mouth of the river is a detached fortification. In it is a large dungeon, so built as to admit the water when the tide comes in. Here the Spanish used to confine prisoners and leave them to drown. In other dungeons they were closed in to suffocate. Some places we have found where they were covered with quick lime and burned alive.[118] Nothing

81

Manila Bay

Light House

Line of March

Puerto en
Proyecto

Port
District

Paseo de Santa Lucia o de Maria Cristina

Large gun
positions

Tidewater
Flag

Plaza
del
Gran
Moriones

Pasig River

San Nicholas District

Co. "A" first fight

Calle Lermen

Calle de Santo Cristo

Meysi

Calle de Jolo

Plaza
Calderon

Calle de Numania

Aduana

Central Manila

0   1/8   1/4

Calle Lecoste

Calle Arranque

Scene of first
fire, Feb. 22,
1899

Calle Anloague

Binondo
District

Santa Cruz
District

Oregon boys
lined up to
receive . . . .

Calle de Escalta

Quiapo
District

Calle de Cabildo

CENTRAL MANILA
(WALLED CITY)

Manila
Bay

N

HQ 2nd
Oregon
Regiment

Calle de Vutania

Moat

Outer Moat

Military
Hospital

Calle de
Concepcion

Plaza Luneta

Manila Bay

0   1   2   3

Tondo

Railroad
Station

Presidio Y
Carcel Publica

San
Miguel

Manila

Ermita

Malata

Paco

Fort Malata

N

Manila Bay

Cavite Area

Fort

was too cruel for these people. The Spaniard is made cruel by education — generations back. The bull fight is the cruelest form of amusement known to modern times — and this is the favorite of Spanish ladies and children. As we see them here it seems as though there was nothing like pity, or tenderheartedness among them. The night I found a sick woman on the street in delerium, the *ladies* — refined ladies — wives of officials — gathered around and laughed at her ravings as though it was the funniest thing out. They never assist the injured or sick. If a man is hurt on the street — he lays there until the police take him to the hospital.

Aside from their heartless cruelty they are very pleasant people — and we get along very nicely.

By this time you are hard at work in school. I know you will work hard and learn lots. So I do not worry. But remember what I said in the start — there are some things not learned in books. Learn to *compose letters*. If you don't care to write to your father when he asks it — do it because it is a part of your education.

Another thing, I want you to remember that you are the man of the house, and I expect you to do your duty. Look after things. See that Mama is not worried when you can prevent it. You are old enough to understand me in this and I hope you will do what I ask.

Your affectionate father,
Geo. F. Telfer

Manila P.I.
Nov 8, 1898

Dear Lottie,

I am still "convalesing." The fever does not trouble me much — but I cannot expose myself in the sun. So I lay around my room and read. Sometimes I will have fever for two or three hours — generally in the middle of the day. Then there will be several days with no fever. I sleep and eat well. Am taking 15 grains of quinine every 3rd day and 3 grains of strychnine daily.[119] I go out evenings. Barber and I usually drive out to the English Club house in Malate and sit for an hour. It is a delightful place on the shore of the bay.

Dunbar did *not* have typhoid and is back from hospital. Gritzmacher did not have small pox and is in from his tent. Kelly was sent to the hospital yesterday with fever. Barber is on duty again. So you see we keep a fair average.

We are in great need of a hospital where we can look after our own sick. We have no money to fit up a building. The government makes ample allowance for food, etc. — but provides no money for stoves and cooking utensils. It will cost about $1,000.00 to fit up a hospital and we need $1,000.00 in addition for contingent. We think of telegraphing the citizens of Portland for the money. The other regiments are arranging for hospitals. The general hospitals are crowded and men do not receive the attention required. If we could have our own hospital — each company would be able to wait on and attend to its own men.

Our officers entertain the California officers one week from Saturday.

Our surgeons entertained the officers two weeks ago.

The companies are all making preparations for Thanksgiving. *Turkeys grow here.*

I enclose post office money order for $25.00 which I hope will enable you to provide a Christmas dinner, if no more. Would send some presents — but fear the duty would make them expensive.

You spoke sometime ago about Povey's promotion. He was not promoted but received a brevet rank of captain on account of excellent service as a clerk in the Quartermaster's office in Cavite. He has not been with the company since we started. At Cavite he had charge of the native laborers, who were unloading the transports. He has worked very hard and has done excellent service. His brevet does not change his relative rank nor increase his pay.

News from Paris today makes things appear war-like again. Anything will be acceptable that gets us out of "Old Manila."

Affectionately,
George

« *37* »

Manila P.I.
Nov. 11, 1898

Dear Grace,

Your letter of Sep 25 with one each from Mama and Willis, was received yesterday via Hong Kong. It seems odd that we are just commencing to hear about what the home world says of our Manila exploit. The *Oregonian* as late as Sep. 28, was received. We get madder and madder as each number is received. This last batch is as bad as the ones before. A long editorial in one tells how superior the regular is to the volunteer.[120] Cites Oscar King Davis as authority to prove that the regulars behaved better than our troops.[121] The only regulars with our expedition were with Maj. Eastwick's command and they made him more trouble than the volunteers. They were dirty and got lice before the volunteers. He had to threaten their officers with court martial several times. Well I suppose we must stand it.

I was glad to get the photographs of the family groups. Mama did not send her photo, as she mentioned — at least I did not get it.

I am glad you find your school studies interesting. That makes a pleasure out of work.

It was very nice that you went to the St. David's hop.[122] I hope you will be able to go to more like it.

The band is located in the room below ours and they practice in concert during the morning and on solos in the afternoon. As you may imagine, it is somewhat trying to the nerves.

It is raining today. That is quite unusual as it ordinarily rains at night and the sun shines during the day.

I will send you a Mauser cartridge by this mail—Manila souvenir. The powder is taken out and the bullet pulls out. Our men fasten them to their hat bands. Doubtless a few bushels of them have reached Portland by this time and you will want to be in the swim. I did intend sending you something in the way of dress goods, but decided that the money was needed at home, and that you could buy what you needed. You will see lots of Manila fabrics soon, and if there is anything you fancy let me know and I will try and get it for you. The Pina cloth you hear of—and which many will have I expect, costs about $17.00 Mex. = $8.50 gold—for a dress pattern. I don't know whether you would like it or not. *It washes*. There are several grades—but only one color—ecru. I don't like to buy such things on my own hook. When some of our ladies get here I will have some one to advise with.

I don't think I shall locate in Manila. At least not until I have returned to America. I haven't the necessary cash capital to go into business here.

There is nothing new to write so I will bring this to a close. I am feeling pretty well. Don't dare go out in the sun, but go out after 4 o'clock and ride or walk on the Luneta. Am not on the duty roster so pay no attention to hours. With much love to all I remain,

Your affectionate father,
Geo. F. Telfer

<< 38 >>

Manila P.I.
Nov. 22, 1898

Dear Family,

The *Senator* arrived today with mail and there is great rejoicing among the men. We understand that our recruits are on board—but have not seen them yet. I pity them when they arrive in barracks. Our men are wanting something to play with and the poor recruits will have a hard time.

I received a letter from Mother—none from the rest of the family. Everybody else got lots of letters. Dunbar received two Kodacs—with about 50 rolls of films. We have three in the room now.

The band is practicing down stairs and I find it hard to compose a letter.

I notice that you put a part of my letter regarding condition of things at the Hospital, in the *Oregonian*.[123] You were considerate enough to suppress names. Most of the officers have got into hot water on account of their friends doing this. But I was in hopes I might be spared. Capt. Davis had to make a public apology to his company for the letter his wife gave the *Oregonian*. His men lost all respect for him (they did not have much to lose) and the officers worried the life out of him. All over the camp you hear—"I can't drill today—have been forty eight hours in the saddle—without sleep." He lied on every proposition. He did not take immediate charge of the gates—but relieved me, after the first twenty-four hours. I had two horses furnished me and I gave them to him — or he would have had to walk. He did twenty-four hours duty — and had a lieutenant to assist him. Everybody here knows this and you can imagine how delightful it was for him to face the guying.

In regard to Whitings letter which is published as a contrast to mine — you know that doctors will never admit the necessity of nurses.[124] They insist that everything is satisfactory at the hospitals — but we know better. Most of the hospital cases are venerial and of course women are not wanted in those wards. But we want separate hospitals for fever patients.

It is interesting to see the mode of treatment in fever cases. The old method of packing is employed — in modified form. A rubber blanket is put on the bed. The patient lays on this. A sheet is rung out of ice cold water and laid over him. It is adjusted so as to come in contact with the body as much as possible. The attendant then takes a piece of ice and passes it over the wet sheet. The whole body is gone over — until the teeth fairly chatter. The wet cloths are then removed and the patient carefully dried — *without friction* — and prepared for sleep. Care is taken not to have the skin get warm. This you know is in contrast to the "pack" — where the object was to get up a sweat. A cool night gown — made in two sections so it can be put on without having the patient get up — is put on — and tied with tapes. A sheet is the only additional covering. He immediately drops to sleep. This treatmemt is repeated whenever the temperature rises. Every precaution is taken to prevent the body heating. In most cases the fever is reduced in a few days. But you never know when it will return. The trouble seems to be getting back lost strength and vitality. Huge doses of quinine are given. Also strychnine. Malted milk is the chief article of food. My lank body is a blessing. My fever never goes to the "ice pack point." I am so thin that I cool off quick. I take 25 grains of quinine every 3rd day now. I eat most everthing but meat. And you know it is hard for me to get strong without meat. I drink a great deal of whiskey and soda. This puts me on my feet and keeps my spirits up — two things hard to accomplish in treating Malarial fever.

I am on duty once more. Went on guard Saturday morning. Did not go through Guard Mount as I do not dare expose myself to sun heat very long at a time. So a sergeant marched the guard to the guard house and I took command there. I stood the 24 hour tour very nicely. Action is necessary to my life you know. I *can't* stay idle in a room and regain health. All our crowd are on duty once more, and I find it hard getting enough food to satisfy the appetite of our mess. Brazee will have to be sent home. He would not take care of himself — and would not diet as ordered. He came back to quarters and stayed a week and had to return to the hospital. The doctors say there is no use in his staying out here.

Private Galloway — son of Auntie's friend — is in a bad way.[125] He has chronic diarrea. Wells is trying to get a furlough for him — or else have him sent to San F. for treatment. He has not performed duty since we came to Manila. He is a very nice young fellow & I feel sorry for him. He looks so forlorn.

A convalescent hospital has been established and is very nice. Wells — who never lets up on trying to have his men taken care of — has succeeded in having three of our boys sent there. We had no one in the hospital a week ago — but have three now.

The Red Cross nurses are doing splendid work. We all wish there were more of them. There hospital is very small.

Cardwell is with Anderson's division and we don't see much of him. His health is better than at home and he is gaining flesh. My weight is up to 130.

Since starting this I have received more mail — Willis' letter of 15th and Lottie's of 16th.

I am much pleased with Willis's letter, that is the way he should write, describe things that he sees. His description of the Railroad smash up was very good. Am glad he and Hazel go to dancing school. Make them practice lots at home.

Wells is working every string to get a commission in the Regular Army. Now that Simon is elected to the Senate I think he may get it.[126] I wrote to Gen'l B. sometime ago and asked his asstance in getting a captaincy in the volunteers, when a vacancy should occur.[127] If Wells gets an appointment in the regulars — of course there would be a vacancy. Gadsby will resign if he can. The Colonel takes the ground that promotions should be made by company. On this ground Barber would get Co. G and I should have L — if Wells went into regular service. I have also asked the General to write Gen'l Otis in my behalf, hoping to get on the list for appointment in the civil government. I might get a staff appointment — but the pay is no more than at present, and it costs all an officer's pay to live when detached from a company. If I get into the civil department I would be in position to hold it after the troops were sent home. How-

ever it looks as though there would be need of all the troops for some time, and that volunteer officers will have no difficulty in getting appointments if they desire to remain here. Beebe and Otis used to be very friendly and if B. will talk to O. as you say he talks to you — I have no doubt it would help me. O. has difficulty in getting competent officers to take charge of administrative work.

Wells has made the best record of any captain here. He is not much on drill — but good on administrative work. Has a good memory and a clear head, and is able to master regulations, orders, etc. He takes good care of his men, and knows more about their ailments than the surgeon. And is the only one who does not snub the lieutenants. If he was not so pugnacious and had smoother manners he would get along better. He and I get along very nicely. I could not get along with any of the others. McDonald and his crowd are like a lot of kids.[128] They drill well — but the whole outfit is far from military. It is "Tom," and "Harry," "Gus," etc. Everything is on National Guard lines.

We are getting ready for Thanksgiving. The two Lieutenant messes combine on dinner. Phillips and I are getting it up. We have 3 turkeys feeding for the occasion. They cost us $9.00 Mex. The whole 8th Army Corps will feed high. Some companies go to restaurants and some have their dinner at home.

Our officers entertained the officers of the 1st California, Saturday evening. The rooms were handsomely decorated. We took palm leaves — ten feet long — and tacked them against the walls. Put lots of flags and Chinese lanterns. The effect was very pretty.

87

Had a native orchestra, 16 pieces. Their playing was grand. I was with the guard so did not take part. In fact I think I am losing interest in such affairs. I always feel fearfully bored. There are very few bright men in this world. I don't think I am very bright myself — but I do like to meet men who are.

Some of these Spanish families must have a hard time trying to live. They are frightfully hard up — and have to sell jewelry in order to get any money. I suppose some of them have friends at home who provide for them. The army officers of course get their pay — when Spain has any money to pay with. But there is a vast army of civil clerks, etc. who can have no income at all. The families of some of the officers who are held prisoner by the insurgents have it pretty hard. Some of our officers have bought diamond rings at very low figures from these people. And carriages — Victorias with 2 horses, harness, etc. — are sold almost daily for $150.00 to $200.00 Mex = $75.00-$100.00 gold.

The friars expect to be expelled and are willing to sell their lands at nominal prices. If one had money there are lots of chances to get hold of coffee and sugar lands at figures that mean a fortune in the near future.

Mrs. Knapp will be in Hong Kong in a week. He has been unable to procure a place for her to live yet. The city is so crowded that one cannot get any kind of a living room. What few hotels there are, are filled, and the people are living 4 in a room. The Reeves have an elegant place at Malate. He asked me to come and see them — to come to dinner. But I have not gone yet. It is hard to pick up society ways after a six month campaign. The officers of the different regiments do not mix up much. Although the Minnesotas are with us inside the wall — we have nothing to do with them — or they with us. It is said here that there are three branches of the army at Manila — Regulars — Volunteers — and the 2nd Oregon. Ours is the only Volunteer organization whose officers "dress up." And our men are not allowed to go around town in flannel shirts and dirty trousers. We require them to have on blouses and keep them buttoned up. We live in fine quarters and entertain callers at mess — or club. For this and other things we are considered "stuck up."

I received a letter from Mr. Miller today. He is with a merchandise brokerage firm in Portland and wants to correspond with firms here with a view to getting business.

Well I have strung out a long letter and said very little. This will reach you about Christmas. I would like to have sent you some gifts — but as I have written before, there is nothing here — except what can be bought in Portland for less money. In my rummaging around I have found a horror in the way of an inkstand made from a skull with a snake crawling out of the earholes. I sent it to Mrs. Clarke — knowing her fondness for horrors.

I trust that you will have a Merry Christmas. Everybody *can* if they will only try. Just make up your minds that you are happy — and you are. *I* will look at my Spanish neighbors and wonder what they are jabbering about. Then I will sleep — or scrap with Barber or Kelley. Sleep some more. Drive on the Luneta. Go to the English Club and sit on the

General Summers and Second Oregon staff
at Manila. (From *On to Manila*)

Dear Family,

I have just heard that a mail goes out today and as you might worry if you did not get a letter, I will scribble a few lines. I am staying with the Red Cross ladies for a few days. This is as much for change of air as anything. It seems impossible for one to get rid of malaria while living inside the wall. This place is outside and nearer the sea. Have been here five days and my temperature does not go above normal. So I think I will go back tomorrow. I am taking 30 grains of quinine daily and light diet. Of course I cannot do much moving about with so much quinine in my head.[129] The surgeon in charge is Dr. Cabell — brother of the Cabell that was National Guard instructor in Oregon.[130] He has been very successful with malaria and all of our officers who have been here are well and on duty now. Ellis seems to lack *force* — does not inspire confidence. Cardwell is with Anderson's Division so I do not have him to brace me up. — It is also good to live among folks. There are 4 women here — all very kind and jolly. Meal time is a special delight. Five officers come to the table — and we have lots of lively conversation.

The Oregon nurses are not here. Miss Killen has a ward in the General Hospital and Dr. Wood is trying to establish a regimental hospital at our barracks.[131] To be candid, I don't think she amounts to much. I don't think she was the right one to send. *I* would

veranda and look at the bay. Will yawn and keep awake until taps, then go to the men's dormetory and take check roll. Say good night to the Sergeant. Come back, pull my net down over my little cot — and sleep until reveille.

There is to be a football game in a few days between the English residents and some of our officers.

Tell Willis that the coat was a musician's. I send him some buttons as requested.

Do any of you wear belts now? I can have some unique ones made here, but don't know what you wear. Also give the length of your feet — in inches — will get some slippers.

Affectionately yours,
George F. T.

have fits if she tried to nurse me. But don't say anything about it. I intend investigating things a little and will let you know the result.

The California crowd turned out poorly — in part, 4 or 5 proved *not* to be nurses. Two were sent home. One man and wife are running a saloon in Manila. One "lady" is living alone and is working up a home for convalescent officers. Supplies sent us care of Red Cross do not reach us. The man in charge is accused of selling some — or using them as he sees fit. Two boxes came with last expedition and Cardwell captured them and sent them to Ellis. A letter to Cardwell gave him the idea that you had sent 6 boxes previous — *which we never saw.* If the Colonel or Ellis had any push we might make a fight and gain something. Of course, we line officers cannot say or do anything.

I have your letters of Oct 22 and 24 which I will answer as soon as I get back to my desk and writing material. All space here is occupied just now. *If you send money for hospital work — send to Col. Summers. You can instruct him to pay the nurses what is necessary.*

Wells says he is getting fits for saying that the men are responsible for a great deal of their sickness.[132] If people at home don't quit censuring officers for condition of men, we will publish a list of ailments and perhaps some of the fond parents would wish they hadn't spoke. The hospitals are greatly improved since I wrote that first letter. Mosquito bars were received soon after, also pillows and sheets. The medical department allows regimental surgeons to purchase foods for men sick in quarters. So there is nothing to worry about on that score.

A convalescent hospital has been established on Corrigidor island at the mouth of the bay. This will improve conditions. There is a shortage of doctors and skilled nurses.

Mrs. Knapp ought to be here in a day or so.

Cultivate all the people who knew or speak of knowing me. I shall need them when I get home. Sorry this letter is not better. I never could write in my lap.

Affectionately,
George

Don't worry about sending me things. I am not in need of *anything*.

« 40 »

Manila P.I.
Dec 7, 1898

CONFIDENTIAL

Dear Lottie,

I am pretty mad. The cause being your letters of Oct 24 and Nov 1 concerning conduct of officers in general and in relation to Emergency fund. It is bad enough to endure the hardships of an expedition 8,000 miles by sea, with all its worries great and small, with its heartbreaking disappointments. To be blamed by superiors for unheard of faults. To listen day after day to complaints of enlisted men — often warranted and often not, but in any case feeling that you are powerless to change conditions. To be dead broke. To be hungry. To be sick. In fact to endure for 6 long months all kinds of trials incident to the command of troops — no one but we officers used to campaigning in the tropics can understand. To go through all this is bad enough — but cheerfully endured because incurred in line of duty. But the last drop was added by Mrs. Jones in her letter to Captain Wells.[133] To show in what light the matter was and is regarded by people in Manila — I was in the hospital when the letter came. I related the matter to Dr. Cabell. Now Cabell is a Virginian — as you know — and the kind of man that is considered the embodiment of chivalry toward women. He left his practice in New York and came here because he considered it his duty. When I told him of that letter he exclaimed — "It is an insult sir!" — I replied, "What can one do? It is written by a *lady*. If it was written by a *man*, one might get satisfaction." He said "Such a person is *not a lady*." Officers and men curse the day we ever accepted that money from the Corps. And any good you may have done is as nothing now. My position is made very uncomfortable owing to the fact that my wife is connected with the organization.[134] I would resign leave here if I could. But resignations are not accepted in this command.

I don't blame you of course. I know you are not responsible for the acts of Mrs. Jones or any other half cracked old woman. It would be useless for me to attempt to prove anything. The word of an officer would not be taken as against that of a half sick-homesick soldier who has been punished for disobeying orders and to get even with the officer — writes a letter to his people conveying the impression that there is a deep laid plot to do him an injury.[135] I will only call your attention to a few points.

In the first place we (the officers) have lived together as one family all these months. Each knows all about the other. We have consulted together on public and private affairs. If one had money he divided it amongst those who had none. So of course I know — or could have known every dollar spent by my comrades. And I will just say that your whole batch of charges and insinuations are *lies* from beginning to end.

Now how much riotous living can be indulged in on $1200.00 divided among 36 men ($33.33 each)?

And captains and lieutenants all had to participate in whatever there was in the way of eating or drinking. One dozen bottles of champaign would cost $35.00. And we appear to have drunk it every day during the voyage.

We contracted, with the owners of the transport *Australia,* for our board on the voyage over—at the rate of $1.00 per day each. This contract was made by Gen'l Anderson's commissary officer. The ship's steward had his own supplies and set our table three times a day—the same as he would if he had been on a regular voyage. Gen'l Anderson's staff and all the correspondents ate at the same table with us—and they insisted on having the best that could be brought from San F. *We* had no money—and Maj. Cloman (Anderson's staff) advanced us enough to pay our bill to the ship—$36.00 each. Now what did we want to steal bacon, vegetables, or canned fruit from the men for? And suppose we did live better than the men? We paid Spreckles Co. of San F. for our food. We could not take Spreckel's stores and give to our men—any more than you could break into a grocery store in Portland and feed a beggar.

Now as to what Platt did *or* did not do.[136] The War Department has inspectors to investigate such matters. Do you suppose Gen'l Anderson would sit day after day and see such things going on and *not* order an investigation?

As to Capt. Wells. *I* had command of Co. L from San F. to Cavite. Any complaints the company had to make—were made to me. I required them to be made in writing. When I was in doubt as to what action to take, I consulted Gen'l Anderson—or which ever of his staff he suggested. In any case I always satisfied the men in some way. An army ration is so many ounces of this and so many of that. Certain things—always specified in army regulations. This may be insufficient in quantity and unsatisfactory in quality—the company officer has no power to change it. He must see that his company gets the full amount of the issue—but he cannot get the fraction of an ounce over. Nobody but the War Department can change that. In addition, certain things in the way of delicacies are furnished the commissary which he may sell to officers and men at a price named in his schedule. He has to pay over the cash at the close of the month for whatever has been sold. Platt had canned fruit furnished him for this purpose. Our men wanted to buy—but had no money. Capt. Wells allowed each man to purchase a limited amount of stuff and paid for it out of the emergency fund, requiring the men to repay the amounts when they received their pay. This was according to a plan agreed upon by us. The idea being to keep the $100.00 intact as long as possible. To do this we considered each sum advanced an individual in the light of a loan. Capt. Wells had nothing to sell and regulation would not have allowed him to sell to men in any case. As for fruit given us at San F.—neither of us ever saw it. Oranges, etc. were given the men on the streets and in their tents—by individuals—but nothing was given to him or myself for distribution.

At retreat tonight I called the company's attention to the charge made against Capt. Wells and left the matter in their hands to straighten. I pity the man who made the complaint if they catch him tonight.

And if any of the Emergency Corps have burning ears tonight — they can trace the source to Manila. You ladies are very unpopular with Co. L just now.

I told you in Portland and I have written from here — that the U.S. Government furnished everything needful for the army. What we urged was for you to bring influence that should compel the heads of departments to send what was required. We never asked you for a cent of money. Your crazy female agent seems to have cabled you that we needed money and supplies.[137] She did this of her own accord. No one from the Colonel down is willing to father the act. We did think it best to establish a hospital of our own and thought it would be necessary to rent and fit up a building. But we find we can make room in our barracks. So decided not to ask for money. As to food for the sick — The nurses and surgeons prescribe the diet of a fever patient. The medical department has all of the foods allowed — and if you should send a million dollars we could not give one man anything different from what he has. The nurses are bothered to death over you sending *jelly*. No sick man is allowed to touch jelly under any consideration.

Soon after Wells and I wrote as to conditions in hospitals — nets and sheets and lamps arrived. Also a supply of woven wire cots. So things are quite comfortable. *But* we are still in need of *trained nurses* and surgeons. We have plenty of attendants — but are short of trained nurses required in care of typhoid. Our surgeons have too much to do and will wear out before long.

Another thing, you must understand that the medical department of the army acts under its own chief in Washington. A chief surgeon is sent here — with a staff of assistants. They run the hospitals. Our regimental surgeons do not have access to these hospitals. They look after sick in quarters and decide what cases should be sent to the hospital. When the man goes there — we lose all authority over him. We are allowed to visit him — but must ask permission of the surgeon in charge. An officer from each company usually visits his men once a day — to cheer them up and to be able to report their condition to friends. We also detail one man to make the rounds daily and see to their clean clothes, etc. Sometimes a convalescent craves a certain food. If this is not on the diet list and the surgeon decides it harmless — we buy it. The men tire of canned milk, for instance — and we buy them fresh.

Now there is one delicate matter which I must mention — Many of the captains do not like to report the precise nature of some expenditures. Something like 40% of our sick are suffering from venereal disease. The men shrink from letting this be known — and do not go to the hospitals for treatment. The cases *must* be treated. The captains frequently furnish the necessary medicines and instruments. This is a phase of army life which is very hard to talk about — but it is our greatest trial in this country where these diseases are so prevalent. In this connection I am sorry to say that our regiment has about 20 cases of partial insanity from self abuse. These are being treated in hospital — and we suspect some who are not in the hospital. Now when you hear of sick soldiers — bear in mind that many are not deserving

Majors Willis and Eastwick dining, second
and third from right. (OHS neg. 77500)

of *much* tender thought. Also have a little pity on company officers who have to keep themselves posted in such matters. We lecture the men and do everything in our power to prevent their contracting disease — but are not always successful. We do not allow them much liberty (out of quarters) — and for this are found fault with.

Capt. Moon sent you a statement in October.[138] I wrote you a letter at the same time. Neither of us understand why you did not get it. (Moon did play 5¢ ante — but *won*.) This game amused officers on the voyage over — but was stopped when we got here. Some of the "poor privates" won as high as $200.00 on the trip. Others were able to loan money to their friends at 4% a month.

One company received *two barrels* of blackberry

cordial. The captain was sick in hospital and the liquor was turned over to the men. They opened it and drank it up in a day or two. What good did it do? If the captain had received it he would have given it out as needed and the supply would have lasted a year — and the men would have written home that the officers had retained it for their own use — and you women would have believed it.

We have a sales depot now — run by Knapp — and all sorts of canned goods, soups, jellies, pickles, etc. are sold at less price than you can buy the same article in Portland. The captains authorize their men to purchase $5.00 worth each — monthly. This is charged the captain and he has to collect the amount from the men.

Capt. Wells is writing his wife tonight — I wish you would ask her to read you parts of it. He gives some particulars I may have omitted.

We think we have got track of the man who made the charge of selling the fruit. If we do he will have to prove it — or else get a dishonorable discharge. I think some members of the Emergency Corps will have to interview the courts before the thing is finished. It is a fight now and everyone of us will fight it out to a finish. I wish you were out of the thing. It seems odd that a wife should be party to a shameful slander that affects her husband as closely as this does.[139]

Mrs. Knapp arrived yesterday. Gen'l Otis declined to receive the money — but had it paid to Lt. Sladen — one of his aids.[140] Sladens people live in Portland.[141] Otis is not likely to treat the matter very patiently.

I rec'd a pkg. sent by Mrs. Knapp. Many thanks.

The pajamas were especially acceptable as I can't get the kind I like here.

I had a letter from Gen'l Beebe. I will write him my opinion of him when I get around to it. His conduct has been contemptible. He and Jackson should have seen that we were protected during our absence.[142] Jackson could have at least explained that the officers of a company have a very small part to play in the affairs of an army corps. He could have explained commissary and hospital regulations.

To show how virtue has its own reward — Platt has been appointed Judge Advocate of Provost Court — with captain's pay.

I think I wrote before that we did not see much of the two Oregon nurses. Miss Killian is in the Division Hospital. Dr. Wood is looking after patients in our barracks. She is not much good as a nurse — being a doctor. She is too giddy for me. She and Crowne are very thick. *We* go to the hospital run by the San F. nurses.

Do not show this letter.

Affectionately,
George

41

Manila
Dec. 8, 1898

Dear Grace

I will try and write in answer to your very good letter of Oct. 22. It is hard for any of us to get our minds down to rational letters, as we are so broken up over the outrageous treatment at the hands of the Emergency Corps. We have dropped almost everything to talk about that. You know we live in a very small world — that of our own barracks — and peopled by our own regiment. So when anything like this comes up, we *all* talk about it. I don't want to talk about it to you — but it is hard to get ones mind down to business. But this much I want you always to remember — never impeach the honor of another until he has had his say. Always assume that a gentleman *is* a gentleman — or that a lady *is* a lady — until you have ample evidence that you are mistaken. It often happens that a person holding an official position — (or in case of a lady holding a high social position) — considers that it is unnecessary to notice the attacks of malicious people. They think their position is sufficient guarantee of character. This is especially true in military life, where an officer is at all times subject to court martial for "conduct unbecoming an officer and a gentleman." And a military court has no mercy.

Well, I am out of hospital, and in new quarters. I have moved to the official residence on Palacio St. — occupied by the field, staff, and captains. I am in a room with Crowne. He and Knapp were together, and now that Knapp is a family man and lives out of quarters, the Colonel gave me his room. I am delighted to have a little privacy once more. The room is quite small — but very nice. Crowne is at the Adjutant's office all day, so I am by myself when I feel so inclined.

Yesterday Capt. Poorman and myself took a trip up the Passig river on the hospital launch.[143] It was delightful. I wish I could show it to you. It is a fact that one knows nothing of life in the tropics until they travel inland on a river. Rice fields, banana plantations, cocoanut groves, bamboo thickets — all combine to form a background. Then a moving mass of color, made up of dark brown natives, poling boats upstream — or paddling down with loads of fruit, hay, and vegetables for market, naked except their waist cloth, every muscle standing out and making them look like bronze statues. On the bank — women in red skirts and white waists. Men in red trousers, children shouting and running — naked. Water buffalo dragging plows or mud scrapers. Queer birds. All combined form a picture that I am not word painter enough to describe. I could only think — "If Grace could only see all this!"

Our recruits are with us now, and the companies don't look quite so thin. Capt. Wells is a little under the weather and I am drilling the company. I am rather weak — and our line is so long — 24 front (National Guard was usually 12) that I tire very soon. The Sergeants are good men and I turn the company over to them when I get tired. The men in the company are very considerate and do their best when I am in command.

Coming in from drill yesterday I picked some flowers — "Morning Glorys" — which were growing on a wall — and took them to Mrs. Knapp, so she could see home flowers blooming in December.

We were advised of Ordway's death when the ship reached Hong Kong.[144] It was of course sad — but we go through so much of that sort of thing that we become rather hard. Of course we regret the death. But we consider one man in the same light as the others. We think of the awful hours of that last day in Portland — the tearful mothers that hung about the camp and begged us to look after their boys. And when one dies — we think of having to meet the friends when we go back. How we shall have to relate all particulars and witness the grief which we cannot comfort. So the son of the laborer is as great a care to us as the son of the rich man. And his death is deplored the same. But our lives are such that death becomes commonplace. The sight of a dead man taken through the street on a stretcher — or trundled along on a cart — does not cause a break in conversation. Only the rich use coffins here. The corpse is placed in a coffin and taken to the grave — and dumped in — the coffin is taken back to be used again. The natives do not even do this — the body is carried on a bier with a cloth canopy over it. As they go along the road — the head and feet are visable and wobble around in a very disagreeable manner.

I was sick on Thanksgiving and ate my soup in my room — but went down and jollied the officers mess while they ate theirs. They had roast turkey with cranberry sauce, escalloped oysters, asparagus, string beans, potatoes, mince and squash pie, shrimp salid — and I forget what else — but it was a swell dinner. (N.B. — the officers did *not steal* these things from the men. We do buy *some* things.)

Some blamed fool here started a subscription to buy a Christmas dinner *for the sick*. They raised $3,000.00. Then Gen'l Otis informed them that the sick would not be allowed to eat turkey dinners. So the money is to be refunded.

With much love to all,
Your affectionate father,
Geo. F. Telfer

My prayer is;
From memory of uplifted eyes.
From shrieks of wounded, battle cries.
From faith forgot when danger dies,
Save us Good Lord.

The above lines were written by a private in the 23rd regulars. It ends a description of a fight, and is a very clever imitation of Kipling — Recessional

42

Manila P.I.
Dec. 12 1898

Dear Mother,

I have been a little might rushed on letter writing of late and have not answered yours in regular course. Daily routine of garrison life does not make much of a showing — from the standpoint of the civillian — but it consumes a great deal of time. And in this hot climate we *cannot* do half the work we are accustomed to at home. I have just aroused myself from siesta — put my pillow out in the sun to dry (*from sweat*) and spent half an hour cooling myself down with a fan. Cold baths are not allowable after noon.

I was up at 6. Roll calls, breakfast, and drills took me to 8. Then bathe and dress. Wells and I put in the balance of the forenoon visiting sick in hospitals and pulling strings to have some men ordered home. (N.B. — "The officers pay little attention to the condition or comfort of the men" — extract from soldier's letter to friends at home.) After lunch sleep was the only possible way to employ time. The heat has been too intense to keep going — that is for anybody but the men who wish to play ball. They keep it up until they get sick — but an officer must keep well as long as he can — so as a rule he does as the surgeons tell him.

You would be interested in the hospitals. The investigations in the east have made the medical department of the army wake up. The result is — plenty of hospital supplies. The men have woven wire cots, mattresses, sheets, pillows, and nets. In addition to the hospital buildings, convents and tents are used. Native servants are employed to do the drudgery, so things are clean and wholesome. Plenty of ice is furnished, so that fever patients can have cool drinks and ice packs in plenty. Every article of food allowed by the diet list is carried in large quantitys. Of course it is pitiable to hear the patients beg for food — as one man told me, "Nothing but corned beef and cabbage will satisfy me."

Mrs. Lawrence Knapp and Mrs. Haynes of our regiment are here. This puts us once more in touch with civilization. We now put on coats when we go to meals, and do not converse across the parade ground, about matters of a private nature.

Quite a number of American ladies are in the city and are objects of great interest to the Spanish ladies. We are picking up a little in a social way. The various regimental bands play on the Luneta evenings, and we all promenade or ride. Our officers attend a reception tomorrow evening given by Gen'l and Mrs. Reeve. I think the next few months will see quite an attempt at gaiety. The houses here are well adapted for social functions. And the large number of men with nothing to do evenings, makes receptions and dinners necessary. As soon as the ladies learn to handle the native servants, more will be done.

The boxes are somewhere in Manila but have not been delivered yet. I will say that I am very thankful for the kind remembrance. I don't know what the box contains — but whatever it is I know lots of love is wrapped with each article, and kind thoughts and good wishes accompany the whole.

The different officers have compared letters — (as usual) and cannot help smiling at the list of articles sent. We seem to have failed to inform our friends as to what we eat, and in consequence are receiving some things *not* novelties. One wife sends her husband 3 cans of gingersnaps — we have gingersnaps on our tables three times a day. We all get canned soups — and we are *so* sick of canned soups and everything else in cans. We live on canned goods entirely, and I think everthing known to the grocery trade is sold here (that is in the way of canned goods). I will try and get a list from the commissary so you can see what we pay for things. Tell Lottie that Mrs. Knapp mailed a list to her sister for the information of the Emergency Corps. Jellies are acceptable — because the factory made jelly contains a great deal of glucose — which is unhealthy in this climate. The sick cannot eat jelly — but the *well* need it. The main thing lacking is *money*. If we have *that* we can purchase what we need. But of course money cannot be had here any more than elsewhere. Clothing — such as we wear here — cannot be procured at home as cheap as here — even if we could get the quality. It takes 18 pairs of white trousers to fit out a man who pretends to dress well. They cost us about $2.00 (gold) a pair. You could not get them in Portland for that figure. Undershirts are furnished us from captured Spanish military stores. When we use these up we can buy from the quartermaster at American wholesale prices. The government sends out everything that can be thought of. Except officers uniforms. If the family was here I could buy all supplies at the price the government pays for them at San Francisco. We have things charged and pay monthly.

The only fault to find is that the staff departments were too slow in getting the supplies to the seat of war. And the ration list for enlisted men was adapted to Alaska instead of the tropics. You understand that a *ration* is what is *given* the soldier to eat. He must prepare it himself. Officers cannot control the matter in any way. The Secretary of War is the only one who can change anything on this list. The officers make out a requisition and see that the men get what the regulation entitles them to. If the soldier does not like the food he can sell it back to the commissary and take the money and purchase from the government store whatever he wishes — the same as the officers do. If we think they are eating food which is bad for them — we make them change. And they are just like children in the matter of good judgement. A man suffering with bowel trouble will eat a can or two of pineapple — or a half dozen oranges. In some cases we have to station a man at the kitchens to prevent certain men from over feeding. We get so out of patience at times that we give it up and let them do as they have a mind to. Then we get jumped from headquarters because our number of sick has increased. It is like being the head of a family of 100 hearty boys.

I am feeling very well indeed. Suppose I will continue so until I get another dose of malarial poison.

I sent Mrs. Clarke a small trifle in the way of an inkstand which struck my fancy. Hope she got it. I don't see much in the way of souvenirs here. That is such as I should value. The men buy quantities of stuff from the Japanese store — which can be duplicated in Portland for less money. Some things in the way of native cloths I have been waiting for female advice before buying. I went shopping with Mrs. Knapp yesterday and she picked out some things which would be valued in Portland. When another payday comes around I will send some home. As soon as the fate of the islands is decided we will be able to purchase lots of souvenirs. *Now*, the insurgents have every place bottled up and we can't get in or out.

Some of the friends purchase novels in pamphlet form price 10¢ — and send out. I have seen several of Kipling's works in that form. If you can find any they will be acceptable. *Anything* standard is acceptable.

Hoping this will find you well and Auntie the same (lots of love to her by the way). I remain your

Affectionate son,
Geo. F. Telfer

Manila
Dec. 17, 1898

Dear Lottie,

Have just aroused myself from siesta. And after a shave, a whiskey and soda, and a speculative look out of the front window — responded to by our Spanish neighbors opposite — I will try and construct a letter.

The box was received yesterday. For days dray loads of boxes have been coming up from the wharf. In order to prevent miscarriage, the Q.M. Dept. took them in charge and the Red Cross manager could not get at it. Our Chaplain looked after our part, and took receipts from each man when his package was delivered. They are still in process of delivery. In addition to individual boxes there are boxes for companies — addressed to captains. It is needless to say that officers decline to receive or distribute these. In our case we turn over everything to the 1st Sergeant.

It is great fun watching the boys opening boxes. We of course laugh over some of the things displayed — but we all appreciate the love which prompted the gift. A great many apples were sent. Some are in excellent condition. Strange to say the article most prized is *candy*. Everybody seems hungry for candy. You know we can't buy it here.

I was much pleased with my presents. Everything will come in handy. The rolled oats and prunes should have been in tin. That is the way we buy them here. I have not tried the soup capsules yet. If they will keep in this climate they will be very valuable. Some of the mess received plum pudding as well as myself — so that we think we will be able to consolidate and have enough for our Christmas dinner.

The underclothes are the right weight for the climate and are an article always needed — for one has to change so often. The table cloths and napkins I will keep until I set up housekeeping. The chocolate I serve out to my friends as candy. The sheets, towels, etc. are always needed. The copy of "A CHANGE OF AIR", was very welcome. The title suggesting many things to a person dwelling in the tropics. Of all the presents nothing is more prized than the photo of yourself. I looked for it as soon as I opened the box. The picture is good. Of course the badge is not popular in our house these days — but as Dr. Ellis said, "We know that there is a good womanly heart *under* the badge." Pardon my not mentioning names in acknowledging the presents — but the tags were lost off — so I will thank you all collectively.

I was at a reception at the Reeve's on Wednesday evening. They have a delightful home and are just as jolly as ever. She asked if you were as pretty as ever. I told her that *I* thought so. She sent a great deal of love to you — in which the general joined.

Wells went on sick report today — and I came off. He has been ailing for over a week — but has not reported sick — but has not commanded the company. Ellis is much concerned about him. He is looking well and is active about the house — but coughs a

Lottie Telfer, during Spanish-American War.
(Author's collection)

The secret service reports the insurgents are on the move, and we see signal fires on the hills within their lines, and fire balloons go up all night. But we don't take much stock in the matter. I drove through their outposts last evening and the sentinals presented arms—and the children shouted "Omega!" (friend or brother). However, we have issued 50 rounds of ammunition to each man and require it to be kept in the belts constantly. My revolver is also loaded and lays within reach. But we never carry fire arms into the insurgent lines. Corpl. Franklin of our company goes home on the *Ohio*—discharged.[145] He said he would go and see you and make a full report of my condition. He has had a hard time of it—and is a fair specimen of a hospital patient. He has been sick in quarters, Division and convalescent hospitals, and can tell you all about it. He is also well posted on company affairs. See to it that he is questioned closely—and by all who are interested. He is discharged and therefore free to say anything he wishes regarding officers of the army. If you can do so—arrange to have him questioned in the presence of Gen'l Beebe. *I* want to *know* that Gen'l B. has heard a true statement—and in such a way that he must acknowledge the fact.

Eastwick sent Gen'l Beebe letters from army and navy officers exonerating him from newspaper charges, etc. These letters were not for publication—but to be used for defense if in the general's judgement it became necessary. *Has* he tried to defend *any* of us? *We know* that he expressed regret that Wells and myself acted in an unmilitary manner in the Pas-

great deal. They are making a microscopic examination of the sputum today. Ellis says it may be necessary to send him away—*Don't mention this to anybody.* It might reach his wife and cause unnecessary alarm.

I have been wanting to go down the bay to Corregidor island for an outing. But the weather is so delightful here that I don't have much excuse for going away.

sig affair — this without waiting for the facts. Since the truth has been published — he hastens to write that I knew all along that the charges were untrue.

It may be of interest to you to know that Co. L receives about $40.00 (gold) per month from sale of savings in rations. This sum (often running up to $60.00) is expended by their mess steward — under the direction of Wells and myself — for articles of food not included in ration issue. They also have an assessment — (arranged for by themselves) amounting to enough to pay a first class cook and plenty of servants to do kitchen drudgery. They are fitting up a mess room now. Have tables built and are arranging to purchase enameled ware for table use and to cover their table with oil cloth. They have a kitchen roofed with corrugated iron, and a large brick range of their own construction. So you see they are not suffering much. The other companies are in about the same condition.

I am sorry that affairs have taken the turn they have. I dislike to hurt your feelings by unkind comments on the people you have been working with. But you must know that we have all been treated so unkindly and have to endure so much in silence — that it at last became unbearable. Col. Summers speaks in the most charitable manner of the whole matter, and insists that the ladies are not to blame. That they have had their sympathies worked upon, and have been wrongly advised by men who should have known better. Eastwick and myself have tried to induce the officers to treat the matter in the same light. We argue that the women have only heard one side of the story, and that explanations written by officers had not reached home when Mrs. Jones made her famous "break." The presence of Mrs. Knapp has helped a great deal. She is such a quiet little woman — that they can't associate unkind actions with her. When they get to talking wild — she looks at them in that same fixed way that Hazel regards people — and they simmer down. Remember that when you enter public life you become a public character — and must take abuse along with a small amount of thanks.

Moon feels very much hurt at you not acknowledging his letter. I have tried to persuade him that you could not have received it when the last mail left home.[146]

Some of the captains (and Lieutenants) return the full ($100.00) — Wells and I talked of it — but as we were dead broke — thought we would pocket our pride.

Kiss the babies for me. And give much love to Auntie and Mother.

Affectionately,
George

« 44 »

Manila P.I.
Dec. 30, 1898

I AM NOT HUNGRY.

Dear Family,

I had hoped to get time to answer each and all of your loving Christmas letters, but have not been able to do so — or if I have been too tired. The little stack of unanswered mail has stared me in the face for a week. I am on a detail as judge-advocate of a general court martial — and the volume of work is almost overwhelming. It does not relieve me from company duty and Wells is unable to drill yet. The court work is liable to keep me for a month. In governing so many men — in a large city with all its temptation, involves a lot of judicial proceedings. However this is a holiday letter and I will tell my troubles to the adjutant.

I ate several dinners Christmas day — and went to high mass at noon. Tried to go to midnight mass the night before — but the archbishop was afraid of the "insurectos" taking advantage of the people being at church — and "breaking out" — so the churches remained closed.

Chaplain McKinnon of the California regiment — as foxy a priest as ever wore black, — arranged for a special service for the army.[147] He preached the sermon — in English. The service was at St. Ignatius — a Jesuit church, as the name indicates. It commenced at half past eleven in the forenoon. Three priests officiated — besides McKinnon. The music was rendered by an orchestra. The finest I have heard since Thomas. The organ was used very little. Being a Jesuit church, women did not assist in the singing — and the singing of so long a service by male voices was very monotonous. I could not find out the name of the composer. One of the features in the music was the constant click-click of castenetts. Whether played to accent time or for the effect I don't know. Then at times tambourines were struck — in a sort of march time. Near the last a beautiful effect was produced by instruments which imitated the singing of many birds. At the elevation of the host, a chime of many sweet toned silver bells on the altar rang, and the chime in the bellfry rang at the same time. The effect was grand. The church itself is beyond description. It is said that there is only one church in the world which rivals it in beauty and splendor of interior decoration. It is not very large — and is plain outside. Inside there is no fresco, nor gilding (except the gold ornaments about the altar). There is no marble — nor the stucco ornamentation usual in large churches. The whole interior is finished in a native wood resembling mahogany. This wood is carved — as only the Philipino *can* carve. The carving alone cost $250,000.00 — in this land of cheap labor. The fluted colums, with their elaborate capitals, the corners, the medalion portraits of the saints (life size heads) are all beautifully carved. It is not polished wood, allowing the use of putty and varnish to cover defects, but rough, i.e. — *natural* — finish. The ceiling is a solid mass of carving — and I could look at it all day, it is so beautiful. The altar is of the same wood

St. Ignatius Cathedral in Manila. (OHS neg. 77375)

polished — said to be the finest ever built of wood. The floor is inlaid wood. There are some very fine oil paintings — in frames of carved wood. There are none of the tawdry ornaments usually seen in Catholic churches. They do not have seats in churches here, you are supposed to kneel all the time you don't stand. But *we* were given chairs.

Co. L had an elaborate "sit down" dinner to which Wells and I were invited. "Sit down" dinner means a great deal to the soldiers. They have eaten on the ground, or on door steps since they started. At last we got them aroused enough to build tables and benches — from lumber furnished for the purpose. Then they took mess funds and purchased blue enameled tableware in place of the government tin. They also bought oil cloth for the table cloth. The table sets under one of the porches — on cement floor. The men brought huge palms and decorated the wall of the building on the one side and the columns on the other. They also had bouquets and 10 foot palms in pots on the table, as they said — "we eat our Christmas dinner in the open air under shade of palms." The dinner was very fine. (They have a regular kitchen now — built a range out of brick with a boiler iron top.) There was chicken pie, potatoes, corn, squash, etc. 2 kinds of cake, mince pie, squash pie, ice cream, sauterne punch and cigars. — besides canned fruit. It was estimated that there was food enough on the table to feed the same number of men 3 days. After that I went to the regular mess dinner — at 3 o'clock. It was very nice. Several of us pooled our presents of plum pudding, Jelly wine, etc. and had a good feed. Then I went to sleep. In the evening Crowne wanted me to go down to *their* mess and get some supper. I was not hungry but went down to see him eat. Their steward had set out a night lunch of cold chicken, lobster salad, bread and butter. Major Willis, Dr. Ellis, Crowne and myself sat down and I was induced to eat.[148] Ellis loaded my plate with salad and told me to eat it — and I did. We drank a bottle of claret between us, and had a nice jolly evening.

The array of Christmas boxes was great. I don't know how many dray loads came. Everybody's people sent things to eat. They seemed to think their boys were starving. The funny part was — that in most cases they sent the same articles that the men object to in their rations. However — everybody was jolly and had a good time. Our soldiers gave the Spanish prisoners a sample of a hot time. The fact that Christmas draws all the christian world close together was never more fully illustrated than in Manila. It was the first thing the two armies had had in common. The Spaniards were trying to celebrate in their way — but as they have no money to speak of — they could only buy a few firecrackers — and sing and dance. Our boys (our soldiers get as much pay as a Spanish lieutenant) got them out and marched them around — with lots of firecrackers, and lots of cigars and filled them up with lots of beer. Mock parades were held — wherein American soldiers acted as officers and drilled the Spanish in American movements. Bands were made of "any old" horn or bass drum. The little Spaniards entered into the spirit of things and enjoyed life hugely. About midnight I heard a racket in a convent and went to investigate. I found some

Formal portrait of Filipino woman wearing native "Maria Clara" style. (OHS neg. 77501)

Spanish soldiers in a room, with a bass drum and one horn, gravely trying to work a tune out of the combination. The Spaniards say they would rather be American prisoners than free Spanish soldiers.

Even the priests ask to have guards maintained in the churches where the prisoners are quartered. They say their officers whip the men and are very cruel. And our sentrys protect the men. We took our guards out of the Augustin church a short time ago and the Spanish soldiers say they haven't had any fun since. Our men treat them as though they were small boys left in their charge.

Sunday
January 1, 1899

A HAPPY NEW YEAR!

The men received the new year with all the racket they could devise. Bands, firecrackers, tin cans, etc. We hear that the President has issued his proclamation annexing the islands. If we can be assured of the fact, it will cause us to more than celebrate today. These months of suspense, cooped up in the city because our government had no right to allow its soldiers to go outside, have been very trying. Even the water we drink is given as a special concession by the "insurrectos". They hold the water plant entire. We can't even look at the pumps without their permission. There will be a pretty "scrap" around there some day.

Some of the officers went to a very swell ball at the Philopina's Club last night. The display of diamonds — as is the usual custom — was fine. One lady wore no less than $20,000.00 value in diamonds.

When I went out for reveille this morning people were going to early mass. When I came from breakfast a while ago they were coming and going to other services. The Spanish ladies look very charming with their lace mantillas — by the way these are worn only at church. Nothing is worn on the head out of doors.

Have been to high mass with Mr. & Mrs. Knapp at the church of San Domingo. Men and boy choir. Music (vocal) cannot compare with Trinity at home.[149]

There is to be a religious procession tonight and we are ordered to keep 60% of our men in quarters and look out for trouble.

I looked up McPherson. He said he had written home to his mother and supposed she would write his sister. I gave him a lecture on the subject and he said he would write every mail. He has not been sick and is a picture of good health.

It is a strange thing that these men who are never sick — are bothered by their people insisting that they are. Every mail the officers have a swearing match while comparing notes over letters — because their female relatives insist that they are witholding information about their health. When a man is sick he is seldom backwards about saying so.

Mrs. Hackney's letter to Mrs. McKinley is a fair sample of the hysterical condition.[150] Our men have never been in the trenches. And never 4 hours without food — or 15 minutes for that matter. Well this is not much of a Christmas letter after all. Will answer your letter later.

Affectionately
George F. Telfer

I AM NOT SICK.

I HAVE STOLEN NOTHING FROM THE MEN (they had nothing I wanted.)

I HAD 1 POUND OF EMERGENCY PRUNES (they were given to me by a non com. If anything is said about this I will send certificate.)

« 46 »

Manila P. I.
Jan. 3, 1899

Dear Lottie,

I am tired and out of sorts tonight. Have stacks of work ahead, but that bunch of letters lays heavy on my conscience and I will let the stern duties of war wait, while I write at least one letter to the dear ones at home.

I did get a Christmas letter off by the last mail. It was not what I ought to have written — but I did not see the time to better it. It was such a cold expressionless letter in comparison to the good ones I had received from you all. But you know my think tank is of limited capacity and it has been on tap for some little time and is nearly dry.

This court martial detail is rather a severe strain on my mental outfit, as I have never been used to courts and their ways. And the defendants generally ring in a lawyer to fight me, so I have to keep humping. Of course you have very little idea of what our courts are like. So I will try and explain — this being a military government all courts are composed of army officers. There are courts for civilians — or all people *not* connected with the army. These courts are composed of officers — but do not try cases where soldiers are to be tried. There are two courts — the Superior and Inferior. Military cases go to the General Court Martial. There are two of these courts under the direction of the Provost Marshal General. These courts are each composed of 7 officers and a judge-advocate. A judge-advocate is like a District Attorney in our civil courts in Oregon. He arranges the evidence, brings the case before the court, conducts the examination of witnessess — *on both sides*, and acts as legal advisor of the court. If the defendant, or any member of the court wishes to question a witness — he writes the question and passes it to the judge-advocate. If the j-a thinks it a proper question he puts it to the witness. If not, he objects to it and tells the court why. Then everybody goes outside and smokes while the court sits behind closed doors and tell funny stories for while. When they run out of stories they toss up to see whether the objection is sustained or not. Then the president rings a bell and everybody comes back to hear the decision. Everything is (supposed) to be written down by the judge-advocate. But after I had written up 5 cases I asked for a court reporter — so I do not work quite so hard. The counsel for the accused is allowed to present his argument, and the judge-advocate makes a reply. That ends the trial, and the court shuts itself up and decides as to the guilt of the prisoner and passes sentence. The record is then sent up to the Provost Marshal General who approves or disapproves the action. The J.A. and members of the court are sworn to secrecy (as to findings) until the P. M. Gen'l publishes *his* say. The court can try a man for any crime and sentence — even to death. But in event of a death sentence the proceedings are sent to Washington for approval. I have not had such a case yet. But I did send one poor fellow to the Penn for 6 months. There are no Notary Publics and the only person who can administer oaths — or acknowledge documents — are the Judge-Advocate-Generals — or of General Courts. So people are after me at all hours to "swear them." I am glad to have the training that it gives me. There is little doubt but what these islands will have a military government for a few years. And of course I stand a show of getting a permanent detail in some courts.

The chief clerk of the Provost office called on me this evening — to acknowledge a paper. Afterwards he spent an hour asking me questions and talking over business. He told me that my reports had been very satisfactory. They had not been obliged to send back one for correction. As he said that was quite remarkable — as most of the courts fail to bring out the necessary evidence. I have also been complimented by defendants and their attorneys for the fair treatment I have accorded them. I am now working up a case where accused is charged with larceny, embezzlement of property, and absence without leave. I have twelve cases ahead — and more on the way. Of course they are mostly "drunk on duty — or on guard," "Disrespect toward officer," or for "disobedience of orders." But some include accepting bribes to pass smuggled goods, assault, indecent exposure, and nearly all the offenses which are incident to the daily life of 20,000 men shut up in a city that never did have any morals.

The court room is on the floor below my living room — so I write in my room and go down to the court room when called. (By the way our residence is called "The Pavellones," Cuertal de Espana. I will

Telfer's first quarters in Manila. (OHS neg. 77400)

have it engraved on my next card. When I tell people where I live they get weak in the knees. When it is fired off—all at one time in the rapid fashion of the Spaniard—it makes a man feel that he has an attack of malarial fever coming on. And when a stranger finds the place, he is apt to expect us to order up wine or cigars to repay him for the mental—if not physical exertion. When court is not in session I drive around to the different barracks and interview prisoners and witnesses. Some witnesses do not speak English so I have to use an interpreter.

I don't know which the Spanish dread the most — our utter (seeming) disregard of danger, our quickness with a gun — or our sense of smell. A Spanish family happy in the seclusion of a Casa Grande — where they have lived for years unconscious of anything out of the way, will be thrown into consternation by the arrival of an American officer who informs them that they are maintaining a nuisance — which smells to high heaven. Our patrols dig up accumulations of filth which would kill some of our home people. Calls of nature are attended to wherever (as well as whenever) it is the most convenient — indoors or out of doors. It is worse among the rich than among the poor for the former confine the deposit to their houses — while the latter go out into the street. Capt. Prescott has been on smelling detail among the monastaries near us. He is a very robust man, but he has to excuse himself from the balance of the party now and then — to vomit. His descriptions make the rest of us sick — so we take his say so for things and do not make personal investigations.

All that you have ever read or heard of these monks is nothing to the real condition. For total depravity I think they beat any record. I am used to a great deal — but they do *me* up.

The Spanish families — the very best — pay no attention to, what we consider, modesty. Children have nothing kept from them. Young girls will watch an indecent dancer, or listen to a lewd song without concern. Women and men make their toilets in front of open windows facing the street. The dressing glass is usually hung on a post which divides the large front window. The ladies can always be seen when doing up their hair.

All downstairs windows have heavy iron bars over them. Young ladies never receive gentlemen except in presence of the family. So all courtships are carried on through the bars. There is a very interesting affair in progress on this street. A young Spanish officer is wooing a lovely Castillian maid with cross eyes — who lives "one block down on the other side." We pass the house on our way to and from the barracks. The young lady is usually looking out of her 2nd story window — you know our windows are really balconies. Sometimes she is drying her hair after a bath. In which case she hangs it over the rail in the sun. As their hair is *all* attached to their scalps — of course her head is in evidence. The young officer walks the length of the block, turns and walks back. Sometimes on one side of the street — sometimes on the other. If it rains he wears a rain coat. His eyes are turned toward that window — she may not be there — but he looks just the same. As there are a great many people passing — he generally has a friend walk with him to steer him along — as he might run into a 6 foot Americano Soldado — who stands not in awe of Spanish dons and might punch his face. I meet him first when I come from breakfast. I see last when I return from taps — 10 P.M. Officers of the guard on their rounds report him at all hours of the night. Sometimes we see him with small packages in his hand waiting for a servant to appear to send it up.

110

He also follows her when she walks on the Mallican or Luneta evenings — with her ma. We are all much interested in the outcome, and smile benignantly on both parties.

A young lady next door to us is engaged to a Spanish lawyer. *She* has a window on the ground floor, and *he* stands by the bars and talks. Some of our officers call at the house. She has fallen in love with Eastwick — all women do. As these women do not see much of the world — they are quite childish in talk. She told Eastwick all about her prospective marriage, etc. Seeing that she was not backwards about talking of the matter he asked how the gentleman managed to propose. Her answer was — "through the bars." So much for social customs, etc.

The 1st California Regiment has sailed under sealed orders for somewhere. And we expect to have more troops move before long. There is no hope for us — the Provost Guard has to stay behind and guard prisoners. What with abuse from home, and sickness among our men and whinings of homesick people, we are about disgusted with life.

I hear there is a mail tomorrow so will close this.

With much love to all,
Affectionately your
George

«47»

Manila P. I.
Jan. 7, 1899

Dear Grace,

I have just learned that there will be a mail at 10 A.M. — and it is now 9, I will have to rush.

The news of Sgt. Morse's death will reach you and you may worry some.[151] It happened, for a wonder, that I was in bed at the time so did not even know of the affair until this morning. There is a Magazine on the wall — in sight of our quarters. There is a strong guard there. There has also been a great deal of trouble on account of insurgents trying to steal ammunition. Our sentries know that in a fight with natives they must shoot quick — or the native will knife them. Capt. Wells and some other officers heard shots there last night and ran over to see what was up. Morse went with Wells. The party scattered out around the buildings and parapet — for the purpose of catching the man who had been seen by the sentry. Morse left Wells and went a short distance — outside the parapet to see if the native was skulking outside. He sprang up onto the parapet and down on the inside within 30 feet of the sentry. The latter naturally supposing the attack was coming from that way — and having no time for identification — in the dark — fired. The shot was fatal and poor Morse died within a very short time. He was not acting under order — nor was he under arms. The officers saw him come over the wall and recognized him — but not in time to warn the sentry.

I feel worse about his death than I would if it had been anybody else. For I thought a great deal of his mother and father — as well as himself. They were among the last to bid me good-bye at McKinley and I was with Morse when he said good-bye to his mother. He was very bright and would have been 2nd Lieut. if we could have got Povey out. I was coaching him up, and letting him drill the company in order to fit him for examination. A great amount of company detail, that would have fallen on me, was performed by him. He is to be buried this afternoon.

I am pretty well — but my stomach gets off a little now and then. Court work keeps me at my desk a great deal — so I do not have to get heated much.

The President's proclamation to the inhabitants printed in English, Spanish and Tagalo was posted up last night. The inhabitants don't know what to make of it. Neither do we. Of course we have not seen the original text — only a translation of a cypher telegram.

We are so disheartened at our treatment by our friends (?) at home, and the disagreeable duty we have to perform here — that we have lost all interest in everything and are simply killing time until we can be sent home.

Tell Mama that the payments from Crocker-Wool-worth bank will close with January, I expect.[152] The arrangement has terminated and we will have to send drafts from here. In case she does not hear from San F. she will understand the reason. Mr. Newhall will probably let her draw just the same. There will be no trouble except the uncertainty of the mails. I will send drafts as soon as paid.

Filipino woman with children. (OHS neg. 77502)

I have lost Hazel's picture. Had it on a screen by my desk — and I think somebody took it.

With love to all,
your affectionate father,
Geo. F. Telfer

« 48 »

(Cablegram as recd by operator)

Manila P. I.
Jan. 8, 1899

Dear Billie Boy,

I have not had time to write an answer to your Christmas letter, — but I have had it in mind just the same.

I don't think the Spanish and Philopena boys have quite the sort of Christmas's that you do. They regard it more as a church feast. Everybody has a jolly time — but there are no Christmas trees or presents.

The slip of paper at the head of this letter is part of a cable message received here from Hong Kong. A long strip of paper passes through an instrument and comes out marked in this way. The operator reads the message from the waves — the same as dots and dashes in the Morse system. The Philopena boys play stick-in-the-hole the same as you do — and holler just as loud. The Spaniards play handball.

Our people played a game of Rugby football against the English residents. We had McDonald, McKinnon and several more of the Multnomah team — but they were out of training and ran out of wind. They were also ignorant of the rules of the game.

We came near winning the Base Ball championship. But Jo. Smith was not quite recovered from a long sickness and not up to his usual play. The result was that Pennsylvania beat us.

On a vacant lot next to our quarters some Spanish and Philopena boys built a stone fort. They put up a flag staff and hoisted an American flag. The Spanish boys then put up a second staff and hoisted a Spanish flag — making one Spanish and one American flag side and side. The Philopena boys protested. And insisted upon having the flag of the Philopene Republic in place of that of Spain. This has led to a series of fights. And every little while some of us have to go down and straighten things out. Last night one of the Philopenas got his head cut open.

The Philopena boys like to play soldier. On the corner of Victoria and Palacio streets is a small park. A lot of small boys have established barracks there. They wear paper caps (not much else as they only wear shirts — no pants) and have sticks for guns. They have a sentry at the gate, and when our officers pass he presents arms just as nice as our sentries do. Sometimes they "turn out the guard" — for our officer. We always return their salutes. It is very funny to see a little mite of a darkey — naked except his short shirt — when at play — stop when he sees an American officer coming, and bring his bare heels together and salute with his hand. We return his salute and then he shows all his white teeth in an expansive grin.

Jan 10, 1899

Aguinaldo has issued his proclamation of defiance — and ever since yesterday noon we have been preparing for a fight. The men slept on arms last night, and the officers stayed at the barracks. I was worn out with court work and my eyes were paining

113

Major Gantenbein and a child saluting him.
(OHS neg. 77391)

me so badly, that I was ordered to *sleep*. So I slept in my room at the Pabellones—with Juan on the floor outside my door and my "gun" under my head. There was no trouble in the night and Juan said when he brought my cocoa at sunrise, "No fight. Me sleep all night." Juan is so determined to go back to America that I think he would stand by me in a fight with his own countrymen.

Our position is to defend the gate back of our quarters. Unless the natives in town break out I don't think we will have to fight. But can't tell. I will close this as I want to have it in the mail if worse comes to worse. I will write another letter later on. I am in no personal danger, so there is no need to worry.

Love to all, In haste
Your affectionate father,
Geo. F. Telfer

114

Manila P. I.
Jan. 15, 1899

Dear Daughter Hazel,

I was more than glad to receive your Christmas letter. I sometimes think my baby is forgetting me. She used to write such nice letters.

I wish you could be here and watch two monkeys who live in a box in our backyard. Our favorite amusement is looking at them. One of them is very timid and when native boys come around, poor monkey nearly dies from fright. But the other monkey protects him as best he can. He runs over and grabs him in his arms and hugs him close as he can and scolds and shows his teeth at the boy.

The two play together like kittens. When they get tired they snuggle up close and put their arms around one another and rest. Monkeys sleep that way— hugged up as tight as they can get.

Most of the cats here are without tails. They look very funny in consequence. Aside from that they are much like our cats at home. As our houses all stand open—the cats walk in and out at all hours. You know I don't like cats very well—and I can't get used to their wandering into my bedroom at night and "yowling."

The monkeys don't make noises when they come in—but they steal anything that is bright—like a watch—or money—or boxes of matches. They have a great deal of curiosity, and if they see you have any-thing in your hand, they watch until you put it

Filipino children. (OHS neg. 77508)

down—then rush up to investigate. If it is a box—like pills or matches—they open it and take out the contents.

The parrots talk, I suppose, but we cant understand them as they have not learned English. Some of them are bright red, some green and some white.

Today is Sunday and I suppose about now you are at Sunday school. I am so thankful that you do not have to live as the Spanish children do. They have no Sunday schools—or anything that makes little girls nice and good. They have Indian women who take care of them and they just sit around—or play. When it comes noon a piece of dry bread is given them—which they eat as they play—on the sidewalk or in the street. About 9 o'clock at night they have dinner. Then—in some family the children play until tired then lay down on the floor any place and sleep. They are never dressed up pretty—even on Sunday. They wear a single short dress with nothing under it. When they are as big as you they have shoes and stockings—that come up not quite to their knees. When they get as old as Grace, they never go out of the house except in a carriage. Only when they are going some place not over two blocks, but then there must be two or three old people with them.

Now you must write me a nice letter to come on each steamer.

Your affectionate father,
Geo. F. Telfer

115

« 50 »

Manila P. I.
Jan. 15, 1899

Dear Lottie,

And still the war goes on. That means, that is, we are confined a little closer to quarters, and are wearing blue flannel shirts. The "insurectos" are always saying that they are going to attack us at some specified hour. As we do not like to assume that they will not — of course we get ready. The fact that they don't attack does not make it any pleasanter.

Of course it would take a repulse of the American line to bring our brigade into action — as we do not go beyond the wall, and the line of trenches is about 3 miles beyond. We have to look out for uprisings in the city and be ready to guard prisoners and keep up the line of communication with the front.

I think Aguinaldo is making a grandstand play with the view of making the American home government think he is somebody and therefore worth buying off. Of course we can do nothing to stop his preparations — unless he fires upon our lines. You know this is one of the annoying things about our system of government. It was always so with the Indians. The officers of the army would know that the Indians were preparing for an outbreak — but the authorities at Washington would order "hands off," until the affair had reached the point where the Indians were ready — then would come the outbreak — and large loss of life. If we could have taken positions a month ago and arrested agitators we could have

saved a war. Now we can't say what the outcome is to be. We know that the delay caused the loss of Iloilo — which the Spanish residents begged us to come and take. We delayed until they were forced to give their city up to the insurgents. *Now* we will have a hard fight to take it.

Aguinaldo has one hundred thousand men confronting our twenty thousand in front of Manila. Only 70,000 of his men have guns. Of course they are not trained in the use of firearms — and therein lies our strength.

Quite a number of the American ladies returned home on the last steamer. This is no place for officer's families at this stage of the game. Mrs. Knapp has been having a run of prevailing complaints — but not seriously ill. Mrs. Haynes is likely to have typhoid. The Colonel had she and her husband moved into our building today. Haynes is laid up with appendicites. They are a pretty sick pair.

An opera company — Spanish — is performing comic opera now. *Mascott* is on this week. They say the orchestra and solo work is good. I wanted to go last night — but the theatre is over town — Escolta — and I could not get leave to be out of quarters. I am still unable to go to Correigidor for recuperation. Think I get along all right here. Only when I am around it seems as though I ought to perform more duty. Ellis gives me a lecture every once in awhile. Says it is very commendable on my part to endeavor to perform the work of several, but that I owe a duty to myself. He says I can only do about so much. He then orders me to lay down and sleep and if I am wanted — not to get up.

116

My room is quiet and I manage to sleep about half the time. When court meets I go down stairs. When a case is disposed of I take a carriage and look up the performers for the next. If I feel good in the morning I go out and drill — if I *don't* — then I stay in. I don't think I get enough exercise. The mental occupation of court work is preferable to mental inaction.

I don't have any returns of fever. Get my usual dose of indigestion — and fall back on banana diet. We all are limp and lifeless — same as Spaniards. I never realized the advantages of stimulants before. When we wake up it seems as though all life had left us. We can't get into action — mental or physical. A drink of whiskey seems to put the whole machine on the move. One is apt to imagine themselves sick at such times. One or two experiences teaches us that we can throw the languor off. The effect of the stimulant does not pass off — if you start up and keep moving. If one is really sick — the stimulant does not have this effect. If we could have plenty of ice, we could keep eggs and milk and make egg nog — but we have hardly enough ice for the sick. The government ice machine furnishes the hospitals. The surplus is supposed to be sold to officer's mess and men's canteen. But those in charge seem to stand in with a big beer garden and sell it to them and will not supply us.

Strange to say, I cannot stomach beer. We have the best American makes — but I don't like it. Wine seems to create too much acid in the stomach. So all the surgeons tell us to drink whiskey. Fortunately we are able to get the best quality.

Some Astoria ladies — the Flavel family — who are "touring" have been here.[153] They visited barracks several times. Also a Mr. Smith — formerly Rosenfeld-Smith Co. of Portland.[154] All Express themselves delighted with the appearance and reputation of the Oregon regiment. Perhaps in time the *Oregonian* will be persuaded to change its tone. Several letter writers have been investigated. They all declare that their letters were "cut" by the *Oregonian* and the meaning changed. The Colonel insisted on one man bringing charges before a court martial — against the officers he has accused of stealing. Promised him full protection, etc. But the man insisted that he had only written some heresay statements — and had so said in his letter — but his whole meaning had been perverted. Our next move will be against the *Oregonian* for libel.

We succeeded in getting Percy Morse started home with the body of his brother. He promised to go and see you and tell how I was. He is a very nice boy — although entirely different from his brother. He was sick a long time and can tell you all about that part of our many trials.

I have a new boy, and he has not learned a word of English. His name is "Bocaccio." If you stand the name on end it is as tall as the boy. He is about 12 years old, and dresses in snowy white, with green velvet slippers. When I walk over to my meals with him three paces behind me, I am quite an event on the street. I have got to go through the long period of schooling that I did with Juan.

7 P.M.

An outpost sentry has just brought in word that colored signal lights are being displayed from a church

117

tower near our quarters. It may mean almost anything you can imagine. So you can fit anything to it you want to. Wells is officer of the day and has gone to investigate. This is a specimen of what we get most of the time. What we always fear is the starting of fires inside the city at the time of an attack outside. That of course means rapid movement of troops and scattering of men. We do not think so much of the fighting proposition as we do the necessity of quick movement. I think we will sleep in our clothes tonight. There will not be anything in the way of movement before midnight judging from the actions which took place during the seige by the insurgents.

Tuesday P.M.

Confound them! They wouldn't fight. I begin to think they don't intend to. Kept everybody in their clothes all night Sunday. Sat up until midnight myself. Then went to sleep with my clothes all on. But it was no use. They did not fire a shot.

Last night I went to the theatre with Dr. De-May.[155] Got home about 11:30 and found letters from home. Yours with the flags — for which I am very grateful. Also one from Grace — Nov. 29. One from Mother — and last but not least one from your father.[156] A queer thing came out of *that*. He used a Park Hotel envelope — with Fond du Lac in the corner. The letters were laying on my desk when he came in. The doctor stood looking at them, and after a while asked "who do you know in Fond du Lac?" After I told him, he asked about nearly all the people there that I had ever heard you mention. As he is a Frenchman — only been in America a few years and supposed to have lived that time in New Orleans, it puzzels me a little. He says he has a brother — a doctor — who lived there for a time. I do not remember hearing you speak of him. *This* Dr. May is not in the army — but is what is known as a Contract Physician. That is a civilian doctor hired by the government.

In regard to Gadsby — don't put *too* much trust in what he says.[157] We learn that he has gone square back on what he promised to do about correcting some errors back home. He came out for the "ad" — as did Moon. Then rushed home to reap the benefit. Don't say anything about this. We notice that he gets great credit for what he did for his company. He had nothing to do with the company. Barber did all the work first last and always. When a man complained of bad treatment, he would say that it was too bad, but being sick himself he was obliged to let Barber regulate things — and of *course* he could not interfere. Thus giving the man the idea that he would have it different if he could.

I am glad that General Beebe is kind to you. It *is* a great satisfaction to have people act that way whether sincere or not. Tell him that he is mistaken in supposing things go through a channel in this army. Personal influence gets us what we want. We never send "through the channel" except papers pertaining to routine work. If an officer wants an appointment he "gets in" with somebody at headquarters and they work it up for him. I was made judge advocate through Platt. If Wells is appointed to the regular army I will get a captaincy on the recommendation of Col. Summers — *provided* the people who influence things at home do not wish somebody else to have it. The Colonel wishes *me to* have it — but we find that *supposed* friends at home do not always let him have his own way. And unless someone at home looks out for us we are apt to be left. Ask Dr. Josephi to use his influence for me — with Gov. Geer.[158] Of course the new Governor does not know anything about me. Jim Wilson could help me if he felt inclined.

There will be a military government here for some-time and I would like a detail in that. You understand *pay* is regulated by rank. If I should be made judge of a court now — I would only get my lieutenant's pay. If I was a captain I would get captain's pay and so on. The advantage in having these details is that surroundings are pleasanter, and one is relieved from irksome details. Platt has a horse and buggy — and a house to live in, all furnished — but his pay is still that of a 1st Lieutenant. So you see that we naturally "*pull*" for the special detail. In case of actual service in the field — of course we prefer to remain with our commands. But at times like the past few month — "*nit.*"

I was very glad to hear from your father. His letters are models of good language — as well as news. I will answer his as soon as I can get time. I would like to give him some idea of the conditions here — and do not care to start in unless I can give full scope to the matter.

Our sick report is down to 90, and 60 of that number only have the mumps.

Moore is right in some respects regarding recovery from Malarial fever. We are *always* liable to its return. But we learn to look out for it and the attacks are not much worse than in the Willamette Valley.

I notice that you have put some more of my letters in the *Oregonian*.[159] Don't be tempted. Too many people are doing this. When anything of that kind comes out — it is generally known who the writer is — (here I mean) and he gets himself into trouble.

Notice the editorial in the *Oregonian* of Dec 2 — on the army question. They say certain things are needed in the way of discipline. In trying to do this the officers of this regiment have been severely criticized by the same paper. Wells wrote to Mrs. Jones that a great deal of sickness was caused by our men refusing to do as told by their officers.[160] This drew a lot of abuse on him. *Now* the same paper makes the same statement that Wells did. *We* have *dared* to do what the paper says only regulars do. And it is all right for a regular — but all wrong for a volunteer.

Wells is a splendid officer — in some things. His knowledge of Regulations and his ideas on hygene and health and disease are accepted by all officers here. All go to him for advice. He has your fathers faculty for going into a subject and mastering it in all its details. I can handle the company as well — or perhaps better — that is, I can "enthuse" the men. But I could never have the energy for paper work and matters of government that he has. He works 18 hours a day. When work gets too thick he asks me to drill the company but never asks me to do any of the office work.

Headquarters of Co. L. Second Oregon Volunteers. Left to right, Sgt. Mouton,
Lt. Telfer, and Capt. Harry L. Wells. (OHS neg. 77395)

Morse's death is a great loss to me. He did a second lieutenant's work. Now a great deal falls on me.

I am glad St. Davids is going to pay you something. You certainly deserve it. Learn to take the credit — but get somebody to do your work for you. That is the way to get on and enjoy life at the same time.

We never hear anything of Hiram Mitchell.[161] What has become of him?

There is a mail out tomorrow morning and I am of course unable to think of just what to say.

One thing — send me a bottle of Tarrants Seltzer apparent — Sedlitz powders will not keep out here. Barber brought a bottle of Tarrants and it keeps

120

nicely. It is a great relief when one gets bilious. Have the druggist mail it for you. They will know how to pack it.

The insect powder you sent is very handy. Mosquitos bite so at night — it is hard to write. A little of the powder burning on the desk keeps them away. Am sleepy, guess I will go to bed and perhaps sleep.

Wednesday A.M.

Nothing new this morning. So will close this letter and mail it. It dont amount to much but I can't stop to write more.

If you see Dan Moore tell him I am going to write someday — but that it is hard to write without saying some things regarding a few people we know. And the "*saying of things*" is not allowed.

With love and kind regards to everybody
Affectionately yours,
George

51

Manila P. I.
Jan. 20, 1899

Dear Grace,

My heart was made glad by the receipt of another one of your very satisfactory letters — in the last Hong Kong mail.

Your grandmother writes that you all seem happy — and that you are the best children in the world. If I can be assured that you show contentment with your lot in life. And that you take up your burdens as they come, with cheerful hearts. That you shirk nothing. That you pass over privations and small troubles — with good grace. That you treat each other kindly. Then my own rather barren life becomes one of contentment. One wants to show something for the years which they have lived. And if one fails in their own undertakings, they have nothing to show — unless their children take up the fight and show promise of ability to carry it to a successful finish. I suppose that most men have a feeling of keen disapointment when they realize that they have not many more years left in which to accomplish anything. This can only be offset by the thought that their children will make records for themselves. And for myself, I can ask nothing better than that my children will spread happiness where ever they may go. I find, among men, that some have the fortunate gift of infusing a spirit of good feeling and contentment in any circle where chance throws them. And I notice that *all love* such men. It is the same with women.

121

Some are not beautiful, not accomplished — not rich — and yet they are welcomed by all, are the center of attraction at all gatherings. I have watched several such people, and am always convinced that it is on account of their happy faculty of cheerfulness, and ability to dispel the "blue" feelings in others.

We still "don't fight." We kill a man or so every night, but that is poor satisfaction. The men are getting so ugly that they use great deliberation in aiming at any person they desire to stop. They will watch a convict for instance, for an hour while he is creeping to a spot where he can make a break. Then just as he thinks he has made it and starts to run — the sentry will send a bullet through him. The other night a native convict was seen climbing a wall. The sentry watched him for a long time, and when he had reached the top he shot him. When asked why he did not before, he said that he was waiting for the man to get into the moonlight so he could take better aim. The *Zealandia* sails Monday and we are trying to get 3 more of our company sick sent home. It takes a lot of work, because so many papers have to be examined and recorded before the order can be issued. This is done in order to have the records in shape in case application should ever be made for pension. There are a great many of such applications in and of course each has to wait his turn. I suppose our kind friends in Portland think it all the fault of the Oregon officers. I wish they could realize how small a factor we are in the military institution. A regimental officer has no more to say about things than a civilian in Portland. All we can do is make an application.

Sometimes we have a personal friend in a department, through which a paper passes and he favors us — that is all we can do.

The following is a list of food allowed a soldier under army regulations; 12 oz. pork or bacon, or canned beef; or 1 1/4 lbs. fresh beef, or 22 oz. salt beef. 18 oz. soft bread or flour, or 16 oz. of hard bread, or 1 1/4 lbs. of corn meal.
and to every 100 men:

15 lbs. beans or peas	4 qts. vinegar
10 lbs. rice or hominy	4 bars soap
10 lbs. of green coffee	1 lbs salt
or 2 lbs tea	4 oz. pepper
15 lbs. sugar	1 1/2 lbs. candles

— This all that is allowed for 24 hours. If the quality is not good or if the quantity is short — then we can kick. But a general commanding an army cannot change the list as published. Allowance is made for the failure of supply in certain articles and other articles are substitued. But not unless the original cannot be obtained. No provision is made for cooked food. Each soldier is supposed to cook his own. Of course they can combine and hire cooks or have one of their number detailed as cook. A cook is allowed 25¢ a day in addition to his pay. A company commander inspects the meal as prepared, and can punish the men if the food is not cooked in a wholesome manner.

You see from this that the men who write the starvation letters home are laughed at by the "regulars." They call them tin soldiers. If an officer eats with his men he has to pay cash for his ration.

The commissary sales department is like a grocery store and any soldier — or officer — can go there and buy what he needs for his personal use. The men can sell a great deal of their ration for cash and use the money to buy other things. But the captain has no say in the matter, other than that, the money is paid to him and he buys what they want. He keeps an account of this money and his account has to be signed by the lieutenants and checked up by a board of field officers. I write you this hoping that at least one person in Portland will understand the position of we officers on the food proposition.

You suggest that I send pictures of myself. My reason has been that every picture of me that has gone home has brought forth the remark that I look "thin" or "bad" or sick. Most of us hear the same thing. Now I am *always thin*. But you generally see me with my neck dressed high. This covers my unusually long neck. Here we dress our necks low, and the cords produce shadows in a photograph, and the general effect is grotesque. Barber took a very lifelike picture of us all one day, in our room. My neck looked 18 inches long — and was very funny. I did not send it on that account. One night I had to "dress up" for a "swell function" — and put on one of the collars such as I wear at home. When I appeared there was a howl went up. It did look funny. It was suggested that I let myself out for a bill board, etc. You have no idea how odd our former style of dress appears to us now. In case anything happens to me you can get a very good picture from the War Department — taken by the government photographer.

Negatives of all of the officers of the 8th army corps are preserved there. Shortly after ours were taken the man was sick with typhoid and the sending of the plates was delayed. I did not see any of them — but understand they were very fine. The War Department furnished copies at cost. They are in groups of course — taken with a very fine camera. I presume they will be published before long in some of the illustrated papers.

From pictures and descriptions you have seen of Spanish soldiers you doubtless suppose them to be very small people. Understand that the Spanish soldiers are recruited from the lower classes. The higher officials are of an entirely different type and are the kind of men that women rave over. They are large, and very handsome. They are fleshy — that is they are after they pass 30. The two classes are a good illustration of one class living high for many generations — and the other class footing the bills and starving in the mean time. The Spanish ladies have the peculiar walk that I so admire in a woman. It is the perfection of grace. They stand erect, and walk in quick time, but not "nippy." They take a reasonably long step — nothing like the Delsarte [162] — and *do not* strike on their heels. I imagine that they could move across a room without jarring the house. They are inclined to too much flesh as they grow older. But always dress trim and neat. Their eyes and teeth are their best features. Their mouths are large. Their long, sharp noses spoil the face — at least from our standpoint. Their hair is dark and about the quality of yours. They take great pains with it. They wash it

Constructing earthworks at a strategic point. (From *On to Manila*)

frequently — and always dry it out in the sun, or open air — before doing it up again. This makes it fluffy and bright. Of course we do not see them except in street costume — which is white muslin.

Monday
Jan. 23, 1899

I must get this off in today's mail so will close. I don't remember whether I wrote you on your birthday or not. If I did not, it was not from any lack of interest in the event — for I had it in mind. With much love to all I remain

Affectionately, your father
Geo. F. Telfer

52

Manila P. I.
February 6, 1899

Dear Grace,

Am somewhat tired out tonight. Got back to quarters at 11 o'clock this morning after two days steady duty.[163] At 10:30 Saturday night heavy firing was heard out at the insurgent line, and shortly after, the call to arms was sounded at our barracks. In a few moments we — Co. L was out at our assigned position by the south gate. And the greatest battle of the present war was under way. The fight lasted until dark last night — Sunday. All night long we heard the firing in an uninterrupted line around the city. Rifle fire, cannon — large guns and small. The roar was terrific. In the morning the *Charleston* on the North East and the *Buffalo* and *Monadnock* on the South, commenced firing into insurgent's camps. This of course added greatly to the uproar. We came in for breakfast, and as the fighting was several miles away — we were allowed to go to quarters. Got a short nap and then packed a few necessary articles in my pockets. Then came another call and we moved out again. Stood around in the sun for several hours. Then came an order for Cos. L and D to go toward the front. We went about two miles out and stood in the sun two hours more and watched the ambulances bringing in the wounded — a cheerful sight. The ambulance men looked like butchers, with their hands and arms covered with blood. Every now and then a

Burned out village. (OHS neg. 77392)

gang of prisoners would be brought in. There was a great deal of excitement of course. Ammunition carts coming in empty and going back loaded, messengers dashing in and out — refugees bringing their belongings — some in carriages and some walking. Every village or church — occupied by insurgents — was burned by our troops as soon as reached. Nothing was spared — so of course the women, children and aged people had to come into the city.

The only work our company did was Sunday — after we stood in the road long enough to feel the sensation of Mauser bullets going over over heads and now and then dropping in the road around us, was to go to a large monestery and capture 1,000 natives who had taken refuge there. Gen'l Hughes had been informed that these people would break out that night and set fires throughout the city and plunder the neighborhood.[164] So, Co. L was sent to hold them. It was rather a tame affair. I took half the company around to the back entrance and Capt. Wells to the front. The people were in the courtyard in the center of the building. The priests told them that if

125

Sharp-shooters of the Oregon Volunteer Infantry. (OHS neg. 77390)

they would behave themselves they would receive no harm. So they were very quiet. We put a sentinel at each corner of the room and at the doors — on the outside. My platoon slept on the floor at the back vestiblule and the others in the front. I tried to sleep the early part of the night — but between the cold (I don't know when I have been so cold before) and the mosquitos, I could not. So I spent the night going from sentinel to sentinel and in among the sleeping natives. Listening for shots on the outside, and watching for a possible rush from the inside. The crowd

was composed mostly of women and children and old men. There were perhaps 300 fighting men in the lot.

There was very little firing at the outer lines during the night — so we knew the Phillopenos were retreating and that those inside would turn "friends" by morning. Sure enough every mother's son of them were bowing to the earth and smiling sweet enough to melt butter. Early in the forenoon people came to look for their cooks and servants who had left them on Saturday — to join their countrymen in the fight.

First they would assure us that the servant was not a fighting man and had nothing to do with the insurectos, then turn and abuse him for deserting them. At noon Monday we were ordered to let the whole lot go and return to our quarters.

Eastwick's battalion — consisting of Cos. C K and G are with Hales Brigade out at the water works and had a little fighting yesterday — we hear.[165]

The fighting is so far away now that we don't hear it, and have settled down to the dull routine of police work. I have my court martial work to look after and don't have much time to think. It was a great battle and the volunteers fought as well as the regulars — and there was no "Teddy" Roosevelt — Rough riders or other cheap candidates for newspaper notoriety to show off.

You will have full accounts long before this so I will not attempt any description. Some of our officers who stayed in the walled city during the fight went out and had their pictures taken, standing among the dead on the battlefield, N.B. — we keep "tab" on some of these people and there will be a "hot time" in Oregon if they attempt to spring any thing of that sort when we get home.

Wednesday
February 8/99

No change. Am feeling first rate. Have caught up on sleep and did not take cold. But I hope the next time I will have time to take at least an extra pocket handkerchief — because when you dress for a hot day

First blockhouse captured and destroyed on February 5th. (From *On to Manila*)

you don't realize that it may get cold by morning.

The mail goes at noon so I will have to close.

The New York *Herald* will have the best account of the battle as they had a correspondent on the ground. The San F. papers pay too much attention to booming California to be of any account.

Love to all,
Your affectionate father,
Geo. F. Telfer

Will try and answer your last letter by next mail. Not much chance of going home while this lasts.

Affectionately, your
George

127

House behind American trench as it looked after night attack. (OHS neg. 77398)

《53》

Manila P. I.
February 13, 1899

Dear Lottie

I have just been informed that a mail leaves at 12 o'clock. I had just laid down to get the first sleep I have had for 24 hours, and am not in shape to write. Will just say I am well. And being 10–15 miles from any fighting—not likely to be hurt.

The particulars of the fighting for the last few days will be in home newspapers before this—so there is little use in wasting paper.[166]

The natives have fought stubbornly and surprisingly well. The generalship on our side has been excellent—and plans have been carried out to the letter. No one is candidate for president—so of course little enthusiasm will be gotten up over our victories. We have shown that we has regiments here that could have fought all around Roosevelt and his so called rough riders. *Fear* seems to be an unknown sensation.

Eastwick's battalion is still out with Hale's Brigade. They are holding lines captured by other troops a week ago while the fighting has worked around to the north—and they don't see much active work.

I have put in the past 24 hours in command of 60 men, guarding Billibib prison-where 800 convicts are confined. There has been a constant fear of an outbreak among the prisoners. I am nearly dead for sleep and cannot think very well. We have a very small force in the city now and it makes it very hard for those here. The men go on guard every other day. I do not have to do duty as I am on court detail—but I take these special details in order to help out.

Will try and answer your last letter by next mail. Not much chance of going home while this lasts.

Affectionately, your
George

<< 54 >>

Manila P. I.
February 16, 1899

Dear Billie Boy,

I was very much pleased at receiving your very nice letter of Dec 29, with an account of your Christmas.

The insurgents are still fighting and we seldom get out of quarters. We can hear the firing at all hours of the day and night. Our lines extend about 20 miles in form of a crescent starting and ending on the bay. Our force is so small that the line is very thin, and if we had not whipped the enemy so hard February 5th & 6th, they would doubtless break through. It keeps the Provost Guard on the jump looking for possible outbreaks inside. It is very hot tonight—but I do not dare even unlace my shoes or take off my leggins. We never know when the bugle will sound "To Arms!."

Gen'l King sent in word at noon that his line was attacked—we were warned to be ready to move out and reinforce on short notice.[167] But all is quiet at the present moment.

Our people have buried 2,000 insurgent dead so far. As the rule is to estimate 3 wounded for one dead, this would indicate 8,000 killed and wounded. Add to this a large number *not* buried, and more carried off by their friends, and many buried in the trenches—where they fell and *not* counted, assures us that over 10,000 have fallen so far. Our losses to date—all told—is 326.

The natives cannot understand how we fight so long without food or sleep. In the wars with the Spanish the fighting never lasted over half a day — then there was a few days quiet. They thought to fight on the night of the 4th and rest the next day. Instead of that we hammered at their whole line for two days and nights. This made them loose nerve and their officers cannot get them to hold together any more. They "bushwhack" us from tree tops and cane patches — but do not give regular battle. The ground is hard and there are so many dead that graves are shallow. The bodies swell and the ground cracks open at the surface and the stench is frightful. In addition to this our scouts are continually finding more bodies hid away in thickets. So you can imagine one of the worst horrors of war.

As each brigade headquarters is moved forward, insulated wire is strung on poles — or trees — and telegraphic connection made with Gen'l Otis's office in Manila — so he can communicate with his generals constantly. In fact everything is better managed than at Santiago. We had many things to contend with — but our generals have shown rare skill — and our soldiers have done wonders. We read of the war on the Atlantic shores now — and laugh. It seems such silly work compared with what has been done here. Of course the Oregon boys feel very sore at being left out, but it could not be helped. *Somebody* had to stay. And as our home people took less interest in us than other states took in their regiments — it was assumed that Oregon would not mind if her sons missed a chance of glory.

I go out with the prison guard in the morning. That means 24 hours discomfort. The prison is in a swampy place and the mosquitos are awful.

I wonder if any of the articles you have read describe the Spanish mode of execution? The condemned person is seated on a bench — backed against a post. A spare iron strap is put over the neck and drawn back toward to the post by a large screw — like a bench vise screw. This strap presses the windpipe until the man is dead. The executioner works the screw fast or slow — according to the amount of money the man gives him. The machine at the prison has operated on 600 people since it was built. Two more have been sent home as relics. It is pretty hard to tell which are the most cruel — the Spaniards or the natives. There is not much choice I think.

I hope you will continue to take interest in electrical works. It is a very good idea to turn ones energy to some one thing. If you will let me know what you need to help you on, I will try and get it for you.

It is hard trying to write letters these days as there are so many interruptions — and it is very hot. So I will close. Much love to all, and be sure and write often.

Your affectionate father,
Geo. F. Telfer

The card is *very neat*.

130

≪55≫

Manila P. I.
February 19, 1899

Dear Lottie,

It is 1 o'clock — and as quiet a Sunday as one could wish. It is hard to realize that there is war all around us. That this hot still day may end in a bloody fight. But such is the case. We live in the midst of constant alarms. The whole command is on constant duty. And if by chance any of us have an errand over town — we go and come as quickly as possible — fearing that we may be needed. Our regiment is heavily taxed — on account of having to furnish so many men for guard duty. Last night at taps there were less than 100 men in quarters. The men do not get over 24 rest — and often only 12. We are taken by company — or detachments — to various places. We never act as a regiment. Eastwick is holding part of the firing line with his battalion — in Hale's brigade. And last night Willis took 3 companies of his battalion part way out, as a reserve. So once in a while the majors have something to do. But the Colonel [Summers] is never called upon — even in council. He is the senior in the Provost Guard — but Fred Ames (Minnesota) was lately made chief-of-police in place of Reeve — who returns home.[168] Summers was ignored. Of course you must draw your own inferences. Gen'l Hughes walks into our quarters — looks over the records, and orders a certain battalion — or company to do a certain thing — giving his order to the

Colonel — if he is there. Of course we all smart under this treatment, but have to make the best of it. The service performed by the command has been excellent, and we get many compliments. Heath has his company over in the tough district, and has unearthed more insurgents, as well as arms, amunition, valuable papers, etc. — in one week — than those before him did in a month.

Our *hard* work will come if there is an outbreak in the city. This is the thing that is dreaded. The insurgent when run down in the field, throws off his uniform, hides his rifle, comes into our line dressed in the ordinary native costume, carrying a white flag — and an innocent smile, calling "Omega" (friend). Is searched for concealed weapons, allowed to pass in, where he joins his friends — and waits for developments. Knives are soon procured and when the time comes — he is ready to fight again. Sometimes he passes the outer line in this manner, and goes to a clump of bamboo where he hid his rifle the last fight, gets it and hides himself in a tree and takes pot shots at the backs of the men who let him through. We hunt him out and instead of shooting him — we allow him to surrender and send him in as a prisoner of war.

We have to allow the native women to come and go at will. Have been searching them for knives. We find the knife hung from the waist — that it hangs between their legs. Hence searching has a certain element of rudeness. This so shocked the general — that he has ordered us *not* to search them. As a result, the men will all be furnished with arms in a day or two.

So you see the fight is likely to continue for some time to come. If we had more troops we could move on and crush the main body, but we can go no further. If reinforcements don't come soon I am afraid we will have to contract our lines—as the men will become exhausted.

It is astonishing how well the men are. Sickness seems to have disappeared. Fighting seems to be a good fever remedy. In our company we have 9 on the sick report—but only two of this number are in hospital, and the balance are able to perform duty if necessary.

The companies in the trenches have no sickness. They have learned how to forage and get chickens and pigs, and how to cook at camp fires—and live like kings.

Of course I fret more or less at having to remain in barracks instead of being out where active operations are going on. But there is no help for it. So I content myself with the thought that I am far more comfortable where I am.

Capt. Pickens, who has been sick ever since we left San Francisco, has at last given up and resigned. He returns home on the next transport. This will give Phillips the captaincy—I suppose.

The Spanish soldiers have nearly all gone home. That is, with the exception of those held by the insurgents. So we are not quite so crowded. As Colonel Summers still insists that we are going home in a month—of course no effort is made to provide suitable quarters for the regiment. He has had this one month idea ever since the 13th of August.

One of the strange things about our government is the failure to provide us with suitable equipment. We have no improved ammunition pouches, for one thing. The men are obliged to carry 100 cartridges. They have the old style web belt which holds from 45 to 50. The balance has to go in the haversack. They must carry 3 days rations. The haversack at best will not accomodate over 2 days—as the meats and beans are put up in round cans—which cannot be packed close. Now take this weight and hang it over the shoulder with a narrow strap—which "cuts" into the shoulder. Then a canteen of water—weighing about 5 lbs. more. Then a blanket—beside the rifle and a man has about all he can carry under ordinary circumstance. The result is that as soon as he gets into action, he has to throw everything away except the ammunition (which puts in his pocket) and the rifle. They put too much weight on the bowels and produce sickness. Modern belts are hung from the shoulders and are like vests, the weight being equally distributed. The English soldiers in India carry nothing but ammunition. Water and rations are carried by carts—or on the backs of porters hired for the purpose. Here even officers must carry all their belongings. In a country where Chinamen abound and where they carry every thing—and wages are low— it seems absurd to punish soldiers by making them beasts of burden—and then expecting them to fight with energy in a hot sun. The usual reply to all this is. *We* did it that way in the War of the Rebellion.[169]

132

Monday morning
February 20

A good nights rest and a bright breezy morning. Have had my bath. Straightened my mess chest. And the "Indian" has mopped the floor. A salute from the flagship announces the arrival of somebody — perhaps the commissioners. Wells is out after news items for his New York letter. Once in a while a shot **may** be heard out on the firing line — but aside from that no indication of War.

We expect Hong Kong mail today. And will doubtless get some month old news. I suppose you are worrying over the war news from here. But you must always console yourselves with the knowledge that we will send cables if any of us are hurt. We arranged to let the *Oregonian* know that we were all right after the battle of the 4th, 5th, and 6th. Suppose they published it — but perhaps they thought the matter of too little moment to give it space. [*See note 166.*]

The young lady next door works at the piano all the forenoon. She is having a session with that Nocturne that you and Grace play. She is just now on a quick step that you play a great deal — I don't know its name. In fact all her pieces are the same as I heard Grace play the last days at home. Music is our *"one touch of nature"* here.

Afternoon

Mail in but I received no letters. But the *Oregonian* gives town news — which is something.

Oregonians with surrendered Spanish arms and equipment. (From *On to Manila*)

Can think of nothing new — or at least nothing of interest to write.

Mrs. Knapp talks of returning home, but nothing decisive. She seems well. All women seem to thrive here.

Mrs. Crowne writes that she sails March 8th.

I hope you are progressing with the boy choir. If the "choir" boys are as much worry as "soldier boys" I can sympathize with you.

Love to all.
Affectionately yours,
George

« 56 »

Manila P. I.
Feby 27 1899

Dear Grace

Your letter of Jan 14th received yesterday. I don't get much time to compose letters now days. When I am idle in quarters there is that restless feeling which prevents getting my mind or body settled down to anything. We never know what minute we may be ordered out on some expedition, and our nerves are strung up to the high notch. I don't sleep much — as I don't feel inclined that way. But yesterday morning — after returning from a 24 hour tour at the prison — I went to bed and slept until 4 P.M. Then I got a full night's sleep last night. So I am in hopes that my nerves are down to normal again.

The insurgents broke through our lines on the north Wednesday night — and set fire to the city on that side. Our company and Co. I were sent over about 3 A.M. As we crossed the bridge leading into the burning district it was about as near like pictures of the place of future torment as I care to look at. The quarter was inhabited largely by Chinese.[170] The Chinamen were being marched out with what stuff they could carry and it was a great sight. The glare from the flames was the only light. Shots were being fired from dark places and from beyond the fire — thus depriving us of the satisfaction of replying. Every now and then a building would be blown up — for the purpose of checking the fire from spreading to our commissary and Q.M. depots. Capt. Wells took

half the company and went around to the further side and I was sent with the other half — to capture a fire engine whose men had refused to work and had locked it up. I found two men in the Co. who understood fire engines, and a few firemen. Had half my detachment leave their arms and act as pipemen. The balance I had guard. Got the horses out, run the engine to the bank of a canal. The men soon had steam up and we were working as nicely as though at home in an ordinary fire. We were all highly complimented for our work — which was witnessed by the General himself.[171] We returned to our quarters at dawn.

I see that you have your own troubles and heartaches. I wish that I could guard you from it all — but every child must grow to womanhood or manhood — with a cross to bear. Each must make their own fight. And the fight continues to the end of life. The old saying — "Be sure you are right — then go ahead" — must be your motto. Avoid all that the world condems. *You* may think certain people are all right, but their actions may be contrary to the ideas of people who know them. Avoid intimacy with such people. You may know them and be friendly but you cannot go into their world or imitate their manners. "He who touches pitch is defiled." This may be a hard doctrine — but it is just. Society must protect itself or it would be chaos. Then you are apt to think they can be a law unto themselves. This is a mistake. Tradition is the foundation. Customs are founded upon tradition. Whosoever attempts to break away from custom will be forever shut off from the society they may wish to enter.

Too much freedom of manner in the company of

134

girls and boys—young men and women is always condemned by good society—however innocent the intent. Late hours, roaming the streets, "gadding," boistrous conduct of all kinds, are bad form. Some of your associates are not the best I know. I don't mean that *they* are *bad*—but their bringing up *is*. Julia may be a very good girl—I don't know. But I do know the history of her family. And the sins of the parent are visited upon the child. This is the law of the Bible—and *must* prevail. Be careful how you take pattern from her—and do not become so closely attached to her—that your name must be associated with her—or her friends. Your grandmother always had an idea of championing wronged people. Don't let her get you into the notion.

Portland ways—especially East Portland ways, are not mine. I expect my daughter to have a character of her own, and that she will be able to rise above her surroundings. I know this may open a rather dull prospect for you. But so train your mind—that you can live within your self if need be. Hazel will come out in a very few years. I expect you to be able to steady her—when the time comes.—I know that you will feel that you are called upon to assume burdens when you ought to be like other girls. But you have broad shoulders. I am very proud of my children—and am certain that they will come out all right. I also know the world—and I know what wins. So I say to you, be patient. Have no friends that do not pass muster with your mother. She may be over strict in her notions—but you will find her right in the end. Stick to school. Education is what counts nowadays. Study human nature. Learn when

Grace Telfer. (Author's collection)

to speak and when to be silent. If your family is cranky at times—don't aggravate matters by unnecessary talk. Keep still. If people are ill-natured—try and head off the cause.

Well I must get up early and make a two mile march so will say good-bye. Keep your courage up and do what is right and I have unbounded confidence in you.

Love to all, and good night.
Your affectionate father,
Geo. F. Telfer

« 57 »

Manila P. I.
March 5, 1899

Dear Lottie,

It being Sunday I will write a letter — as a matter of form. It is hard to think of material for anything. We hear firing now and then but it is a long way off and we can't see what it is about. The streets are very quiet on account of so many soldiers being away, as well as most of the Philopenas. Everybody is required to be off the street after 7 P.M. — except American officers and men on duty.

My own amusement consists in going out to the Presidio prison with a guard twice a week. Mrs. Bean, the major's wife is a very jolly woman and sets a good table.[172] There are quite a number of officers near there and we have very pleasant times. Aside from that we stagnate as usual. Talk about remaining in the army! Nit. The life perhaps appears delightful to the outsiders — but the outsiders don't know of the exasperating things in a community where "rank" is everything.

We are having dry weather now — and it gets very hot during the afternoon. At night we have to sleep under blankets. Our blood is very thin and as soon as the sun goes down we feel the change. A lot of the guard were shivering around at camp fire at early dawn the other day. Some thought it cold enough to make thin ice on water. The thermometer showed 70°.

A lot of ladies came out on one of the last trans-ports — but Gen'l Otis will not allow them to land. Mrs. Willis was allowed to spend one day on shore with her husband last week. I suppose they will have to go home. The ladies here may also be ordered away. Mrs. Knapp talks of going anyway. Gen'l Otis has no use for women in campaign. It takes nearly a battalion to guard the women that are here now. Half a company is required to guard Gen'l Anderson's family alone.

I received a letter and a package from Mrs. Clarke. Please thank her for me. I will write myself when I wake up enough. She sent "A Desert Drama" by Doyle. It is especially interesting to us out here.

Platt was married a few days ago.

The failure of the Hall bill means that we stay here 6 months or a year longer.[173] On the strength of this Crowne and I cleaned house today and rearranged our room. It is almost a year since we entered the service. The time has passed quickly — at the same [time] our home life is a vague — far off thing — like a dream.

Gen'l Beebe writes to many of the officers and promises to assist them in getting into the army. He says he knew we were all right all the time. Pity he did not express some confidence when we needed it.

Tuesday evening

Guy Jennings of Co. L returns by the next transport. I will try and get a package ready to send by him. Jennings is a boy that I think a great deal of, and I would like to have you cultivate him. He was operated on for appendicitis, and finds that it will be 3 months before he can perform duty — so his father procured his discharge.

Lt. Haines who was operated on for the same trouble — a week ago — is getting on nicely. One astonishing thing is the rapid healing of wounds. You would suppose that this climate would be a hard matter to contend with.

Eastwick's battalion has had a little fighting this week. Three men wounded — but no deaths. There is some talk of one of the regular regiments relieving us and our going out to the firing line. I don't care much. The majors and captains get what little credit there is in these affairs and the lieutenants do a great deal of the head work — and get no mention. So I don't enthuse over the prospect of living in trenches and getting very dirty, when there is neither honor nor glory.

Friday night

The 17th Infantry arrived today and have orders to occupy our quarters. We are packing up and expect to move to the front in a day or two.

I have held this letter in the hopes of getting a check to send with it. But we have been so rushed that it could not be done. So will get it off by itself.

Mrs. Knapp left us today.

Will close this and get it mailed and will write again Sunday.

Love to all
Affectionately,
George

« 58 »

Manila P. I.
March 12, 1899

Dear Lottie,

Have just got this pay check #81523 — $100.00 and *about* time to get it in the mail. Have been on guard all night and everything is mixed up — packing. We join Anderson's division tomorrow — Wheaton's Brigade.[174] Love to all

Affectionately,
Geo. F. Telfer

My birthday I observe.

Native huts used by Americans. (OHS neg. 77378)

Tents used during marches; their absence is mentioned in Letter 59. (OHS neg. 77503)

《 59 》

camp at Malapat-na-bato near Pasig P. I.
March 16, 1899

Dear Family,

Left Manila on my birthday and marched to San Pedro Macati and camped in dry rice field for night. Rain. No tent. At sunrise moved into line of battle on left of line and moved toward Guadeloupe. Our regiment being the pivot — the right of brigade swinging to left so that our line encompassed the insurgents and driving toward Pasig river. Laid on face in mud behind knoll most of morning — to keep from bullets. Battery in front of us made lots of noise. Could see whole line as it advanced. Reached river in afternoon of 13th March up road on river bank to present position where we camped for night. Morning of 14th march taken up toward Pasig. Enemy made strong resistance and we did not go far. In afternoon Cos. L and B were placed on bluff overlooking part of Pasig — facing north east so as to fire on rifle pits on east bank of Matco river — 1400 yards distant. This to keep insurgents under cover while wagon train moved up road — also the advance of a part of 2nd Battalion toward north — on north bank of Pasig river. Stayed there until last night — when we returned to our present camp. We are resting while the General is figuring how to cross the river. Wells and I occupy a thatch hut — native. Rains about half the time.

Am feeling well and the bracing air of the hills is driving malaria out of our systems in great style.

Pasig was captured yesterday.

Affectionately, your
Geo. F. Telfer

139

« 60 »

Camp at Malapat-na-bato
March 17 1899

Dear Family,

We are still camped—or bivoaced in "any old thing" that will help shed rain. We have very little in the way of personal baggage. Nothing aside from cooking outfit was allowed on wagons. The men and officers carried their own baggage and ammunition. We protested on the first days action, as our men were so heavily encumbered that they could not move over uneven ground. But only 7 bull carts were given the 7 companies. We started to form line and the men proceeded to throw away their blankets and tents. We had them piled up in a field and went on without them. When we reached the Pasig river road, the wagon train passed us—for the two regiments of regulars on our right. One regiment had about 20 carts. They carry tents for officers and men—cook tents—cots—desks, and in fact every thing used in a camp. However the Quartermaster was ordered to send carts enough to bring in our baggage from the field. Now we have two bull carts for each company. One carries cooking outfit, the other the blankets and shelter tents. So when we receive orders to camp—the carts drive in and we unload and use our ingenuity in fixing shelters. The hardest part is to keep the blankets dry. Or to dry them out when they once get wet. Wells and I get a native hut when we can. When we can't—we put a rubber blanket on the ground and one over us and sleep as best we can.

The generals don't seem to have formed any particular plan for the future, so our "Flying Brigade" is roosting just now. The climate is glorious and the rain comes only night and morning. So we all enjoy life. Yesterday the men went on a foraging expedition and have been living on chickens, eggs, ducks, and young pig.

March 22

On the evening of the 19th we were ordered to get ready for the return march to Manila. But the regulars got lost among the insurgents and not knowing how to fight them got badly done up. Prescott's company being near by was ordered to their relief and at 8 o'clock P.M. we were ordered to move forward to be ready for a fight in the morning. So we struck camp, loaded our carts and were ready to march in less than 30 minutes. We march 2 miles and bivouaced in a rice field. My rubber coat was my only bed. At 4 A.M. we got up and had breakfast. Wells and I had a present of a case of Frankfort sausage (canned). And two sausages, a hunk of dry bread and a cup of hot coffee was all I had to eat until 7 P.M. We stripped down to as few articles as could be got along with. At sunrise the regiment moved out in single file up a trail over the bluffs—*following the same trail that Wells, Heath, Prescott and myself followed on our memorable trip to Pasig in July.*

As soon as the summit was reached we united with

A Company of the Second Oregon getting their "firsts," "seconds," and "thirds" behind the trenches. (OHS neg. 77439)

the 22nd Regulars who were camped on our right, and the Washingtons on our left. Then we proceed to sweep the country toward the lake. It was a long thin skirmish line. The men standing at one pace intervals — no support or reserve.

We march over hills, through dry rice fields and bamboo thickets for about half an hour, then the enemy open on us — and the battle of Laguna or Baby [Laguna de Bay] opened. We would lay down and fire, then get up and advance. As we advanced the enemy would retire and it became a foot race. The native can run faster than we can and we could not get within 1,000 yards of him. Our only show was to head him off. We ran up hill and we ran down.

River gun-boat *Laguna de Bay*. (OHS neg. 77385)

Sometimes we were allowed a five minute rest. The Washingtons got in on the enemy flank — but the d — -d regulars could not get around to head him off before he got out to the hills on the south end of the lake. In fact the regulars could not keep up with the line. The big mules which were hauling the artillery gave out and the men dragged their guns by the drag ropes. Gen'l Wheaton said, "The mules have given out, my horse has given out — but the Washington and Oregon volunteers go right on." It was very hot and the advance was the most rapid known since the civil war.

The last half was made at noon — at the lake shore. We had moved steadily since 6 A.M. — over ground that cannot be equalled for hard marching. Our hands and feet were cut and torn by thorns, and we were blackened with powder — ashes from the burned rice stubble. The men suffered for water — for the awful fever, which comes on in action, parched their throats. Of course they had canteens of water but they were soon empty. Of course it was beyond human endurance and men commenced dropping out after the first hour. I stood it until the last hill. Then I weakened from my waist down. The fighting was over and I thought it better to stop before I got too much exhausted. So I camped by a clump of bushes, poured a little whiskey into my folding cup and filled it with water — I did not drink much water during the advance. Then I wet my handkerchief and washed my face and cooled my head. Then I considered my chances of standing off any stray party of Indians who might seek to gather me in. I had not used my revolver, so had a belt full of ammunition and I decided that they would have a hard time getting me. After a while I saw two soldiers struggling along. I blew my whistle and called them in. They were badly winded. One had a bad headache and I fished out my vial of Phenastine and in half an hour had him all right. Then I commenced collecting stragglers. I called in every one I sighted and soon had a party of 15. They were not much good to march but they could all sit down and shoot. And I knew that we could stand off any force of insurgents near us. After an hour's rest I ordered a march toward the lake — following low ground. A messenger overtook us and told me that the command would march back by the road along the lake. So I was able to get ahead and have half an hour's rest before they came up. I took the men to the beach — had them take off their belts, etc. and try to sleep. I learned that there were a number laid out in differant places and decided to wait for them. A few of my party were able to join their commands as they passed. This was at 1 o'clock. I told the others that I would not move until 3 P.M. — and to *sleep*. At 3, I started and had 27 men. It was a sorry looking crowd but the sleep cured the exhaustion and my being all right in the upper story, I was able to keep up a running fire of banter. We halted every half hour and rested. We burned every house we passed — which had been overlooked by the main column. About 5 o'clock we reached the town of Taguig where two companies of Washington troops were quartered in a convent. It happened that one of them was the Vancouver Co. They had been foraging and were at dinner. They took my men in and filled them up with chicken dinner until they could hardly speak. I drank a cup of hot coffee and ate 4 small squares of hardtack — about one ounce. We also got some clear, cold drinking water. Then we pulled out for camp *via* Pateros. We had to cross the Pasig river on a canoe ferry, but I caught the regiment at the point where we bivouaced the night before — and was only *one half* hour behind them.

Found Wells dining off the hind end of the bull cart — and discovered that I was hungry. I ate much hot baked beans, bread and coffee. The striker then spread my poncho and blankets on the ground and I took off my tired shoes and tried to lay my bruised feet where it was softest. Then I thanked the man who discovered that cigarettes were necessary in the tropics. Wells and I lay on our backs while the sergeants gathered around and we told our day's experience and enjoyed ourselves until we dropped to sleep — watching the Southern Cross which twinkled and winked its four star eyes at us through a clear atmosphere. At 7 the next morning we took up our 8 mile march back to Manila. We are now camped on the shore of the bay and Wells and I have our tents on the same spot where the company picture was taken when we first came, and within the shadow of the flag we saluted when it went to the staff head on the 13th of August — and the world was informed that Manila belonged to *us*.

Strange to say I did not have an ache nor pain. Aside from the raw spots on one of my ankles — I would have nothing to remind me of that awful march.

Captain Wells. "He takes good care of his men . . . he is the only one who does not snub the lieutenants." Letter 38. (OHS neg. 77504)

9 P.M.

Have just received orders to march at noon tomorrow. Eastwick's battalion came in tonight — so the 2nd Oregon is once more an entire regiment. I presume we go north to take part in the operations around Malolos. This being Aguinaldo's capitol, promises to be a hard struggle.

On Saturday I received Grace's letter of February 6 and Lottie's of February 8. It is late and I have lots to do, so must close.

With much love to you all I am
Affectionately yours,
Geo. F. Telfer

«61»

Camp at Malinta P. I.
Monday March 27, 1899

Dear Family,

Have a few hours breathing spell — but am too tired and rattled to construct a letter. We had the left in the charge Saturday morning and the company got pretty well knocked to pieces. Wells with the left of the company, got cut off by swamp and I started over the trenches with about 40 men. Water and mud on one — and a continuing fire from the insurgents on the other side of that putting a cross fire on our left and 5 lines of trenches on our front. Heavy brush and timber on our right prevented concerted action.

Kelly in command of Co. A was on my right and we fought it out on our own hook. Capt. Heath commanded the battalion. He and we dropped out of sight right after the first command and he did not see us again until we came into position at the finish. It was a second Balakava — only the insurgents were too rattled to shoot straight. It was a move unlooked for by ourselves as it was said that no body of men could cross the space between the two lines — our trenches were within 100 yards of each other. We were ordered to jump over our trenches and charge — and were not given the usual volleys before hand. The insurgents in the first trenches did not have time to realize what we were doing and retreated as fast as we reached them. We gained our position on a ridge facing Malabon, and the insurgents fired at us across a bayou all day.

Details of the fight you will get later. But as the Oregons do not stand in with the press — especially at home — you will hear what cannot be repressed. The associate press dispatch last night contained the words — "The Oregon regiment charged gallantly" — and the *censor* cut out the word gallantly. So you will be able to judge of correctness of the press reports. But the German consul and other foreign officials who saw part of the movement and have looked over the ground — say that it was one of the most wonderful feats of modern warfare.

I came out without a scratch, although reported killed.

Wednesday
March 29

Did not have time to continue this, as received orders to return to Caloocan. When we got there our Co. was divided and I took 25 men and came to the place where I am now and relieved a company doing outpost duty. Capt. Wells took the balance to occupy a block house. We are both just outside the city of Manila.

I am on the shore of the bay and maintain a line of pickets to prevent communication by rebels. I am a "post commander." I occupy a house and my flag — the one you sent — floats from my window. Will write later.

Affectionately,
George

Malabon Trench. A section of the bomb-proof trenches captured by the Oregon Regiment at Caloocan, March 25, 1899. The dirt embankment in front was ten feet thick and eight feet high. (OHS neg. *77370*)

《62》

Gagalangin P. I.
March 28, 1899

Dear Family,

This is the place I was in when I closed my last letter. It is a town. I did not know that it had a name until today. Our troops burned it a few weeks ago — all except a few residences. The inhabitants, being insurgents have gone hence. I am mayor of Gagalangin now. My official residence is in the second story of a chicken coop. That is a regular thing in this part of the world. The building would make a fair play-house for Miss Muffit and Jane. The chickens live on the ground floor, and the floor of my room is made of bamboo slats. An ambitious young rooster with a high tenor voice — feels called upon to an-nounce the fact that he is alive — at midnight and at sunrise. His place of rest is under my bed and consequently I am apt to wake up at the hours mentioned. My people are largely Chinese and engaged in fishing. There are also some salt works, and a large lime kiln. These important industries are not in operation at present. The Chinese put in most of the time following the army and pilfering the camps. So we "hold up" every one of them and take away contraband articles. I levy toll on the fishermen and get enough fish to feed my men. My main occupation is sleeping, eating, and looking out of the window. The window fronts on the main highway — but as traffic is somewhat light these days — I don't see much. The Dagupan R.R. passes about 1/4 mile away — so I hear whistles and the rumble of trains once more. I have an outpost out on a dike and go out to inspect it twice a day. My command — consisting of 25 men have a pretty good time. They have good shelter and little to do. They fish and paddle around the lagoons in canoes.

My landlord is a very bright young native. The female portion of the family are not here. The man waits on me and cooks what food I do not get from the company kitchen.

We go to a deserted mansion nearby where there is a fine large bath, fitted with shower and take solid comfort getting cleaned up. I sent to town and got my cot and mosquito net, and a clean uniform. Shaved and appeared a gentleman once more. I was a sorry looking object when I came. A week's growth of beard. Sunburned. Had not had my clothes off nor washed. Had laid in mud. Waded streams. Slept on the ground without bedding. So that when I saw myself in the glass — I hardly knew which one of the party I was. But "Wheaton's Flying Brigade" is *the* thing these days. And the officers and men who were on the left of line March 25th, have the entre of society no matter how they look. The small silver bars on the collar of the blue shirt is the only distinction between officer and private. We do not carry swords. A stick is used to indicate directions and for signaling.

Sometime when I am a *G.A.R.* or something like it — probably I will be able to give a minute description of what *I* did, but I don't know much now.[175] No man can make me believe that you can hold a company down behind a breastwork for 15 minutes — with bullets just skipping the top of it — then jump over into the thick of the fire, keep his men lined up and in position while advancing over 5 lines of trenches — and know much about what is going on any place else. I know I commanded, beseeched, swore, belted with my stick, threatened with my revolver — to keep those men in order.

I passed my own wounded men — and saw them as one would look at a person laying by the roadside if they were looking from a window on a swiftly moving train. I remember jumping trenches — seeing mangled bodies, writhing figures, and hearing groans — seeing blood everywhere. But through it all but one line of thought was in my mind — "Guide right." "Preserve touch." "Advance" *"Lay down"* "Forward" — *"Kill" "Kill* — "Take no prisoners." — Then dropping — out of breath and panting. Wetting my handkerchief from my canteen and cooling my head. One queer thing did come to me in the very thick of

147

Soldiers' graves, Paco Cemetery, Manila. (OHS neg. 77382)

the charge. I had tied an enameled tea cup to my canteen strap. Putting my hand back I discovered that it was gone — and looked on the ground to see if I could find it. The loss annoyed me as much as it would have done at any other time.

During the remainder of the day the fighting was at long range and I was back moving about in the woods and under cover a great deal of the time. I went back over some of the ground covered in our charge. The position of the dead insurgents impressed

148

me more than anything else. They wear a blue and white pin stripe cotton uniform. Straw hat — and are barefooted. Most of them were shot through the head. They mostly laid as if asleep. One man who was near my postion for several hours laid on his side — feet toward me. He looked exactly as if he had curled himself up for a comfortable nap. Once in a while I would look toward him and wonder how long he was going to sleep.

Friday
March 31, 1899

Still in same place. Firing on the right indicates fighting toward Malolos. Our regiment will not be engaged for some time.

Tell Auntie that one of our company named Taylor was killed Saturday.[176] He came from Jacksonville and spoke of knowing she and Edith. He was with Capt. Wells when their party was cut off. Was shot twice — but lived some little time. The party were under heavy fire — Taylor laid with his lower limbs in the water. The Captain staid and fought until he died — as they could not carry him. Then they retreated and it was the next day before we could recover the body. We kept firing in that direction and prevented mutilation of the body. He was our "striker" and the men had guyed him about being cold footed — consequently they feel badly over his death.

An officer can *have* no feeling. It is awful to see men you like drop by your side and not be able even to *feel* sorry. You can't stop for mercy — as the *greatest*

On the hike to Malolas in April 1899, Oregon Regiment. (OHS neg. 77441)

good for the greatest number must be thought of first. If you do stop to think you become unnerved. Besides it is wrong to have favorites. A man is waiting to take this to town and I must close.

Much love to all
George

«63»

Gagalaugin P. I.
April 2, 1899

Dear Lottie,

Easter Sunday—and as peaceful a Sunday as one could expect to pass. It has been very hot—but our usual afternoon rain did not come. At sunset I went out to my cossack post on the dike and watched the tide go out for a time, then had one of the men paddle me back in a canoe. The water was like glass—clear out on the bay. The effect of the sunset was grand. The gorgeous colors in the sky, the reflection in the water, and the dark outlines of the mountains across the bay made a combination that would fill an artist's soul with joy.

There has been no fighting all day—so the calm has been complete. The men had a fresh meat issue and my fishery produced a big lot of fish and oysters—so we had a big feed.

I have had you in mind all day and imagined you with your choir—anxious and working hard. Also thought of you in a complete state of collapse when your day's work was done. I think I would rather take a company of soldiers through a battle than work as you must with those boys. I am very glad that the people express appreciation of your work. While I detest flattery—I do consider expressions of appreciation for work well done—the greatest reward that can be confered.

One of our men who was wounded in the fight of the 25th reported back yesterday. He said that there was nothing that did more good in the hospital than the visits of one woman who did nothing but go around and talk to them. She is a Mrs. Russell—wife of one of the surgeons. I met her just before we left Manila. She is very beautiful and has a sweet voice. She told me that she was useless as a nurse—but felt as though she must do something—so put in her time visiting the wounded. Now that would seem a senseless proceeding—but it calls forth more expression from the men than anything that is done for them. So it is—if one can only find out *where* they might shine—and *shine* there instead of trying to do something that they are not adapted to.

I have been living with a crowd so long that I get very lonely being by myself. In fact yesterday I was quite homesick. I can't get away or I would go into town now and then. I sit in my window most of the day and watch the natives who congregate around my domicile. They chatter in Tagalog and try to be social with me—but as I can't understand them we don't make much progress. But they afford me some amusement.

Marilao P. I.
April 7, 1899

I have moved since starting this. The company is reunited and with A and M with Heath as battalion commander. We are guarding the railroad—or a part of it. This station is about 15 miles north of Manila and south of Malolos. We are camped in a dry rice field near the railroad track. The town is about 500 yards west of us. It was a very pretty place—but most of its nice residences have been burned and its church partially destroyed. Regimental headquarters are about 6 miles south at Malinta. Some companies are on the road north. Wells made a reconnaissance today and found the insurgents about 3 1/2 miles to the north east. He had about 50 men and did not dare attack. We look for a fight in that direction tomorrow. Although we are on an open plain (and the sun comes down awful hot) there is a fringe of beautiful trees all around us. The Bocane river is on our right and we have good bathing. And when we wish, we go and sit under the wide spreading mango trees. Wells and I have a 9x9 tent fly—which I have extended by use of bamboo matting on poles. Although the sun is very hot—a cool breeze blows from 2 P.M. until sunset and makes life endurable. The nights are always cool—so that we need our heavy blankets. The men are developing great ingenuity in the construction of shelter. Some have huts built of corrugated iron roofing taken from burned buildings. Some have torn down Nepa huts and built shantys. And some are using the regulation Dog tent. There is plenty of rice straw so they have good beds. We don't lack furniture. We find that any place. I am writing on an inlaid center table and sitting on a Vienna chair such as you have at home. We have a rocker and a bamboo arm chair. Wells has a regular bed. I prefer my folding cot. I have a tent made of a sort of muslin which draws over bamboo bows at either end and I am mosquito and bug proof.

We perform no duty during the day—but put out pickets at night. Scouting parties are made up from volunteers—every now and then. It is great fun for the men to go on "nigger hunts." The air would be delightful were it not for the odor from dead niggers which have been left unburied.

Everybody keeps well and the men are all very jolly. The constant change and freedom from the monotony of guard and police duty is what they like. Our rations are not adapted to the climate—but we forage and manage to get enough to eat. Being on the railroad we are able to get fresh bread and now and then meat and vegetables. Wells had some germia sent him in his Christmas box—and we make our breakfast on that—with bacon and bread and coffee. At noon we have soup and bread and coffee. Or, if very tired I made beef tea and chocolate. At night we have bacon, fresh meat—or chicken if fortunate enough to get one—potatoes with gravy—bread and coffee. If on the move we live mostly on sardines and canned sausage. Incidentally I eat prunes—they are both filling and refreshing and can be carried in the pocket.

We received some Krg-Jorgenson[177] rifles today. So now we can reach Mr. Nig. at his own distance—2000 yards. As it has been he could shoot at us and remain out of range of our rifles. But we are with a general now (Wheaton) who thinks nothing too good for the Oregons and he sees that we are not slighted.

I will mail this for I may not get a chance to finish tomorrow.

Love to all
Good night
Geo F. T.

George F. Telfer house from 1899–1901, 402 SE 30th Portland. (Author's collection)

Residence of Emmeline L. Telfer, George's mother. (Author's collection)

《64》

Marilao P. I.
April 14/99

Dear Lottie,

Am sorry you are having so much trouble about family matters.

If you think you would be more contented by living by yourself—you had better move. Of course I regret conditions but cannot change them. All I ask is for you to be sure you are taking steps that will result in the greatest happiness as well as contentment—to yourself and children.

Affectionately,
George

« 65 »

Marilao P. I.
April 14, 1899

Dear Family,

We are still guarding railroad. Also it is still hot. All efforts to induce the natives of the Province of Bulacan seem to be of no avail. The commissioners proclamations, printed in Spanish and Tagalog — offering every inducement for them to return to their homes and occupations. They returned — but. The fun commenced about 5 days ago. I went out with 13 men to scout toward the east. I found a very rich country — thickly settled. I treated the people nicely and they were very friendly — and had nothing to do with the insurrection. Having gone 8 miles and turned north and crossed the Rio Marilao intending to return on the other side. The water was very deep and we had to cross on a bamboo raft two at a time. When the last two were about to come over — the natives opened fire from a trench on our front. I dare not retreat on the raft — could not advance and the river bank was a jungle of tangled bamboo and trees. There was nothing to do but crawl through. We found a caribou trail and forced our way along as fast as we could — keeping the timber between us and the natives. After a two mile scramble we came to a stone dam and were able to cross back. As soon as a habitation was reached — we stopped to rest. I was so used up that I laid down and took a nap. In little less than an hour we started home. Just as the last man started, the pursuing party crossed the dam and opened fire. We could not stop to fight as we were enclosed by timber on 3 sides. We retreated until we came to an open — then turned on them and soon forced them to cover. Then we resumed our march homeward. There was about 40 against our 14. That night the insurgent forces moved on to our lines and made a concerted attack — I had fallen onto the left of their advancing line. We heard firing north of us during the night. As it was not near us we went to bed and to sleep. At 3:30 A.M. we were aroused by the cracking of rifles and zip of bullets. Our outposts had not given us warning and we were surprised. We tumbled out behind the rice dikes and fired where we could see flashes. It was pitch dark and the racket was so great that it was very hard to direct our fire. The rice dikes here are about 10 inches high and we had no other protection. We laid on our faces when not shooting. The thing lasted about two hours — when the insurgents withdrew. In the meantime they had cut the wires on either side of us so we could not communicate with headquarters. Four men who were patrolling the track were cut off and 3 killed. One played 'possum and escaped — badly wounded. The next day we proceeded to devastate the country. We burned every house within two miles of our camp — and drove the natives away. At noon Col. Summers and balance of regiment came up on train and picked up A and L. We went about 10 miles where we camped for the night with the 13th Minnesota. Gen'l Wheaton arrived and took command. Some artillery also arrived. At daybreak we started for Sta. Marie — an insurgent stronghold. Aguinaldo was there with about 1,000 troops. They made slight resistance and then retreated. We burned the town and every house or rice stack near there. We marched back to the railroad leaving a trail of smoke such as this country has never seen before. We shot at every human being that came within range — paying no attention to white flags. We took train at about 3 P.M. and returned here. Yesterday we commenced fortifying the camp. Our company is on one side. A on the other and M on the track. I am bossing trench building on our side. The men think it pretty hard work. We have plenty of chickens to eat in consequence.

The men who kicked at not being allowed to go out and fight are getting their stomachs full. War is nice to read about — but is not enjoyable.

We get little news out here. Cannot get away long enough to go to Manila. I don't know whether Mr. Lewis has arrived or not.[178] Presume he would remain sometime in Hong Kong.

I received letters from you dated March 6 — last week. Will try and answer some day.

Affectionately,
Geo. F. Telfer

« 66 »

Marilao P. I.
April 21, 1899

Dear Lottie,

We are under orders to go north from here tomorrow afternoon, with 10 days rations. So I suppose there is to be a "nigger hunt."

We are in a provisional brigade with the 13th Minnesota — Col. Summers commanding brigade.

Am feeling well.

Forgot to mention in my last that the China boy Wells and I had for a packer — went into the village looking for stray caribou and did not return. We found his body two or three days after with his throat cut. This within 500 yards of our tent. We burned the village afterwards.

Lieut. Young laid down under a tree near camp.[179] He had one foot drawn up and the other leg crossed over so that his foot was as high as his head. A Philipini took a shot at his head from behind and shot off his great toe. This within 400 yards of his tent. This will convey some idea of the comforts of our home. When we go out to bathe in a creek nearby we take an armed escort.

Hope this will find you all well and happy.

Affectionately,
George

154

67

Maosin P. I.
May 5, 1899

Dear Family,

We are still on our march northward. We draw ten day's rations. March 2 days halt 1—march 1 then wait for another 10 days to come up.

We captured the little city of Bustos a few days ago. It is a beautiful place—one great grove of bananas, betel, cocoanut, and mango trees, with houses hidden away in the shade. 8 of us had a beautiful residence with nice grounds and were very comfortable. We had two nights of sleep and a day and a half good feed and rest. Then we were ordered on to this place to protect the front—while the army waits for rations. This little village contains about 50 Neppa huts. 8 of us occupy one 10x12 in size. It is very hot and the rainy season is on. We have no life nor ambition.[180] Feel bum. The army is not adapted to the climate and if it were not for our foraging we would suffer. As it is we live largely on rice, corn meal. We have some canned corned beef and a great deal of bacon from our own stores. Also coffee. I had some tea—but that has given out. I have a can of prepared chocolate which may last us out. Wells, Heath, Kelly and I are messing together just now and as we are all partial to cleanliness—and good eating we manage to keep in good condition. Heath has a native servant who waits on us. The mango season has commenced and we eat all we can get. This fruit does not ripen on the tree—so it is hard getting it as we do not stay in any one place long enough to ripen it. The fruit is picked and packed in straw to prevents its heat or bruising. The insurgents gather up everything as they retreat—but sometimes we are quick enough to get a little. At this place we got over 100 chickens, lots of hulled rice and sugar. I keep well—but suffer some from constipation.

I heard from Lewis the other day. Col. Yoran met him on the train from Manila to Malolos. I wish I had that bottle of Seltzer apparent.

We are now looking forward to a regular battle. Yesterday we made a reconnaissance in our front and found the outer line in front of San Miguel. We estimated about 1500 men—entrenched. Of course we have small fights or skirmishes daily. We loose more men from heat prostration than from bullets. Although we have been a year in service, Alger has not been able to furnish a uniform suitable for service in the tropics. We have no sun helmets—wear the regular campaign hat—with no neck or spine protection.[181] The sun is directly over head and no shade. The men wear blue flannel shirts, misfit brown overalls and contract shoes. Nothing fits. A man wanting #7 shoes is apt to get #9. And many have their feet tied up in rags. The insurgent shows up in a neat fitting blue and white cotton uniform with a wide brimmed straw hat on his head. Our men are paid when convenient—not oftener than once in two months. The insurgent is paid every month. He is well armed and has plenty of ammunition. We have a few good rifles and 15 different kinds of ammunition. Frequently in a fight our men discover that their cartridges will not fit their guns.

Oregon Volunteers driving Insurgents out of Tondo. (OHS neg. *77387*)

May 7,1899

Still in the same place. Still hot. Still damp and steaming from the sun's heat. We scout some in the morning. The balance of the day we lay in our huts and curse everything and everybody. The general commanding is not sustaining his generals in the field. Columns push out into the enemy's country expecting to unite at certain point — or supported from the rear for purpose of keeping open communications — but after reaching exposed or advantageous positions find that the other or expected column — has been ordered back by telegram from Manila. Lawton's division is now laying idle at and around Balinlaug.[182] Summer's provisional brigade (to which we belong) having been pushed out to this advanced point is stranded. Our objective is San Miguel — only 8 miles in advance. We are against the outer line of defense — and left. It was supposed that McArthur's division would advance from the west and all forces would concentrate on the objective. We have listened day after day for McArthur's cannon on our left — but hear nothing. The enemy comes out and shoots at us now and then. We have no defenses — but lay right out exposed to any shot sent in our direction. *Now* we learn that the enemy has reoccupied all the towns we captured on our way out — and we are likely to abandon the attack on San Miguel to go back and fight over the same old ground. We could have gone through to San Miguel and back in the time wasted. This is of course irratating — when taken with the weather.

Strange to say I have developed the greatest appetite I have known for a long time. I am hungry an hour before each meal — and eat so much I feel uncomfortable. Of course during battle or skirmish we don't get much. In fact if we eat much when hot or tired we throw it up. I put 4 hard tacks in my shirt pocket and a can of sardines in my trousers. My canteen of water completes the repast. While the prunes lasted I put ten of them with the hard tack. We always have our kitchens up for breakfast and supper. Wells always says that he does not eat much and will carry nothing — except his 4 hard tacks — but is always ready to help me eat whatever I carry when eating time comes.

We have a one-horse covered cart called a carametta and our personal effects are carried on this. As soon as we camp this comes up and I have my bed sack and mosquito tent. And if it rains, the Pup tent. We get our meal from the men's kitchen and take canned goods from our private chest to fill out.

But when we stop a few days we live in a house — or hut — and have regular "sit down" meals 3 times a day. Capt. Heath and I like tea better than coffee and today were able to purchase a supply and are happy.

Mail came today. I received another letter from Gasport. Lizzy says she has a collection of tea pots and would like one from the Philippines — as she has one from nearly every part of the world.

You may think it strange that I do not say more about home matters. I cannot make it clear why. But I think of you all and have your welfare at heart. But when one awakens with bullets making holes in the

157

In the trenches. (From *On to Manila*)

roof. And has to have a guard out when take a bath. Sleep with their clothes on and be ready to chase the festive Googoo out of your camp in the night. And with it all, wonder whether you will be shot at from the next hill when on the march, and whether you will be hit or not. With all this — somehow home affairs seem remote and hard to discus. So don't feel hurt when I don't say anything rational. This campaign cannot last much longer and then I will try and say something.

Must cut this off at once as mail starts back.

Affectionately,
George F. Telfer

68

Manila P. I.
May 27, 1899

Dear Lottie,

We returned here day before yesterday. Do not know when we sail for home as there is talk of detention by Medical Department on account of exposure to small pox.[183] I may get home as soon as this letter — but write on a chance. Am quite well with exception of diarrea — which hit me a week ago. Am taking the starvation cure. Only eat every second day. I have coffee for breakfast, beef tea for lunch and dinner. I get awful weak — but as I have nothing to do, it don't matter much. Two letters from Grace and one from you with your photograph met me here. Was very glad for it had been a long time since I had a letter.

We are the heros of Manila at the present moment. Mr. Lewis met me — was at the train when we came in. Also brought over the candy — which was fallen upon and eaten up very soon. We all crave sweets. Our regiment was treated with great consideration by Gen'l Otis. The old quarters being the finest in the city were ordered vacated for us. The 10th Infantry occupied them and thought permanently. The wives and families and officers were all settled — but had to pack up and move. Crown and I are in our old room once more.

I suppose by this time that you are settled in your new house.[184] I hope you are very happy. Undoubtedly the move was for the best. I am more than glad that you have the bicycle. Have not had a chance to

American patrol starting out on their daily rounds. (OHS neg. *77373*)

talk with Mr. Lewis yet. Will try and find him this afternoon.

Affectionately,
George

<< 69 >>

At Sea 375 miles from San Francisco
On board S. S. *Ohio*
June 11, 1899

Dear Family,

I will write this in order to get it in the mail as soon as we land. We expect to get into port tomorrow afternoon.

You will observe that I am on the *Ohio*, and may notice from reports that Co. L is on the *Newport*. I was detailed Quartermaster on the *Ohio* and as the company was assigned to the *Newport* we separated.

We have had a most delightful voyage. Not a case of "Seasick" reported. Lt. Col. Yoran is in command of the two battalions. I have the commissary department as well as Q.M. — so I am the "main guy" of the ship. Regulations allow me the great privelege of standing on the bridge — where none but the ship's officers ever go — except the commanding officer of the troops. I also have a special stateroom for my use. But as the wind blows and it is cold on the bridge I never go there. And as we were crowded and two officers have their wives along — I gave up the stateroom. But I can boss the whole ship — and you know I like to boss. I have excellent sergeants in charge of departments and a paid clerk to keep my accounts. So I mostly read, sleep — or look at the water.

The load of the ship and stowing of men and giving every officer the best stateroom kept me pretty busy at first. And I will have a few lively days in San F. getting unloaded and moved out to camp.

159

Return of the Oregon Regiment to San Francisco on July 7th 1899. (OHS neg. 77505)

At Nagasaki I had to take on 10,000 lbs. fresh beef and 20 tons of ice. This kept me on ship two days out of the three that we were there. But I saw lots of the town and partook of a Japanese dinner. I also mingled with the Geisha (not spelled right) girls. Like many traditions of the east they are not what they are "writ." I think Matthew Arnold was a "mark." It is not best to write everything I saw — because it will make the telling of it stale.

My health is improving rapidly and I cannot hardly realize the sufferings of the past three months.

I suppose Portland is mad because the regiment was not sent there.[185] Many wanted to go — but it would cost the regiment $40,000.00 and the "out of town" officers and men said that they did not care to contribute that much toward a Portland show. Besides the feeling is very bitter toward Portland — and the state for that matter — on account of the attitude of the *Oregonian*. And few care to go to Portland in uniform. They say that they must behave when in uniform — but when in "cits" once more they can "scrap." — I get about $150.00 more by being mustered out in San F. than I would in Vancouver.

Have not had a letter for two months. Hope one will meet me at San F.

Affectionately,
George

«70»

San Francisco
July 19, 1899

Dear Lottie,

Will try and scribble a few lines to send with Draft for $150.00 which I hope will help out. I don't like to run myself out of funds until we start home as it costs money to be a returned hero. *Darn this hero business anyhow.*

The Portland crowd is increasing daily. I wish you were here — but don't think you would see much fun in it. The weather is too cold to enjoy anything.

Your letter of 17th just handed me. I will not stop to discuss the question of mustering out. I could not have changed it if I had wanted to. Gov. Geer puts the matter very well.

I moved to camp night before last. Got tired out talking to people at the hotel. Have not finished my detail yet. Will hold onto it so as to be free from company work. I go and come as I see fit — Annie came out the first day and left a basket of fruit and an invitation to dinner — which I did not get until two days later. Have seen none of them yet. The Rawleys all came to the dock to see me. Have not had time to look them up yet. I am Col. Telfer once more — that is, the Portland crowd make it so. I get satisfaction at being able to swell a little and patronize some of the officers who have been ranking me — rubbing it in a little too much. More of this later.

This must get to the mail so will close.

Love to all
Affectionately,
George

Appendices

1506 Taylor St.
San Francisco
May Twenty-sixth, 1898

My dear Mrs. Telfer:

After a *long* silence (yet not in thought) I write to tell you, I had the *great pleasure* of having your good husband dine with us, on Monday evening, previous to his eventful departure. When I read his name among, the officers, in S.F. paper — from Oregon, I felt *I* must see him, for old times sake —

How strange ones heart goes out — to the hero — whom we have no idea, of meeting, under such circumstances. I did not know whether your husband, would know me or not, yet for your sake, and his mothers, I sought his familiar face — felt so glad to know , I had not been "*forgotten.*"

Well Sunday, I sent Mary to Presidio to invite him to dine — Monday eve — was indeed, sorry, when Mary returned, and said "the Camp may be broken up Monday eve — but if not "Lieut [*sic*] Telfer would gladly come." He did, however — and I can *assure*

you, dear friend — I shall always bear the last dinner event, in mind. He ate *heartily* — was so brave, and looked upon his going to war with such true manhood — All our folks were so impressed with his ideas of war. He left some touching remarks, that will never be forgotten by us. His soul, spoke out — his confidence, in Providence appealed to us — and of all — his *tears* — when he spoke of "Mr. Dave Dunn" whom I know well — in this way, it seems Mr. Dunn had been to camp — night before breaking up, and Mr. Telfer said he hoped to see Mr. D. at the train, "to cheer them up with his happy face etc" — and Mr. D. said "Telfer I'll do more for you than that — I'll pray for you!" Such coming from a man like "Dunn" broke me all up — then the uncontrolled tears, rolled down the manly breast, of your soldier husband — Mrs. Telfer dear. We all felt a choking — it was a sacred moment — so sincere had the feeling been. May good Mr. D. Dunn's prayers, be heard in this great war — as with ours and other, God must grant the noble sacrificing, men of America, victory! And I hope and pray the dear ones of Oregon, who have

163

allowed, a sacred family member to go forth to battle, even though a heart string, is almost broken, the sacrifice may be doubly rewarded, in their safe and speedy return. I must congratulate you dear friend in being so brave — how could you dear?

Louise, Non and a young friend, and myself, went to the *Australia* yesterday to see the troops get off. Mr. Telfer — was out to luncheon with a gentleman friend of mine — whom he met at dinner, previous evening and taking a *great* liking to your husband invited him to lunch! He returned later, said he had a fine lunch! I am so glad he got off to go — for I am sure the Camp lunch did not satisfy one — I shall never forget, the troops filing on — the boat; such few people were allowed inside the wharf, (but *I* am always fortunate,) that the poor soldiers, I think for the first time realized the step they had taken! Up to this time all had seemed a "picnic." It was of course to be expected too as the "homeleaving" seemed to be in their minds, your husband and Capt Davis, and other, viewed it from a different standpoint, they as men — knew what they were doing — but younger men — I fear — did not — I was indeed surprised at the attention shown the Oregon Companies, in good things to eat. The officers will not suffer — they will have the *best*, but the poor soldier boys — I fear will suffer — in their stomachs. The outgoing of the "Transports" last evening was a scene I shall never forget. *We* have a fine marine view from our back windows, and when cannons boomed, and whistles blew, we ran upstairs and saw such a sad, solemn sight — to us — a perfect procession, three large majestic steamers — five tugs, and a large ferry boat,

with a smaller one — taking passengers to escort the troops to the "G. G. Gate." I know San Francisco is a most generous City in doing the proper thing — and as this is the center for all troops to leave — *we* feel *war* is with *us* — I feel certain our home boys — and Calif. boys — are faring better. The Nebraska ones — are suffering — as they are just being looked into by the good people — one [or] two states have been shown the first attentions, but as the brave ones — are gone first — the others will get their just desert. We all feel though not *directly* interested that war is right here. I wish you could see, and hear, the boys being fed three times on wharf, yesterday bet. 12:30 and 4:30 — and hear their hearty yells — as the "Red Cross Ladies" took their departure. There is far better discipline and training in Portland Co. — than in any other so far — Newspapers remark it. I can not think of any thing to write you of except the war excitement. I promised your good husband, I would surely write you that he was "well — and as brave as a man" and had "an excellent appetite." Said "this will please my wife and mother Mrs. Raleigh." Please tell dear Mrs. Telfer Senior — I am sorry she had to see her only child, and son go to war if she regrets it, but if she is proud of his heroic action, I congratulate her, I fear *I* could not be so brave — Harry is anxious to go as an artist, but luckily he is under age.

I can scarcely believe dear "Gracie" is a young lady — how I should love to see her — I saw dear Hazel — when in Portland three years ago — and Willis too is grown. Well eight years makes many changes. Our love to them. Non and Louise intend writing them. Give my warmest love to your dear

Mother-in-law tell her I regret not seeing more of her three years ago.

May God bless you dear friend, and give you courage — to bear your brave husbands absence. And may God bless his mother and grant you both, a speedy return of husband and son.

With hearts best love and sympathy
— I am as ever your sincerely fond friend

Margaret T. Raleigh [186]

Manila P. I.
Dec. 8th 1898

Mrs. Geo F. Telfer
Portland, Oregon

My Dear Madam,

I have just received your letter under date of Nov 1st 98 requesting a statement of my account with the O. E. C. of which you are the representative of Co. "C", it gives me great pleasure to comply, and I have presumed to end my association with an affair that has been a source of unjust and unwarranted annoyance to me since about the first of Oct. at which time I first learned that I had become a thief. Also I wish to state that this is my third statement to you and it occurs to me rather odd that you have as yet received no word from me, in explanation of my enclosed statement. I have purposely drawn a balance on Aug 2nd showing that I had expended not only the original $100.00 but $26.90 additional and on the date of that letter to the Eugene Guard, July 14, you will observe that there had been expended for the Co. $95.08 besides which I had loaned in cash to members of the Company $23.40, the first money, or pay received by any member of the second Oregon was on regular pay day for the Regiment August 8th 1898.[187] I make this last explanation to show you that the statment "that Officers appropriated the funds to their individual uses, and reimbursed the fund when receiving their salary" is untrue. There has not been the slightest foundation for the stories that have gone home, in connection with this matter, and I can only account for it, as being a feeling of jealousy, on the part of those few who have written, and the natural depravity to be expected from a *poor soldier*. There are men, and true, in the 2nd Oregon but they are not writing libels home, to excite sympathy and strange to say they are *excellent soldiers*.

My dear Madam, I am writing plain in this letter, and allowing you to understand how I feel. I left as good a little wife in Oregon as ever blessed a man's life, but the people there have not spared her. They have been unfaithful, hard, quick to condemn men they have known for years, and those dear little women left widows for they know not how long must be constantly reminded, that while the husband who is absent, has always been honest and trustworthy, he has fallen ignominiously for a paltry one hundred dollars, and under circumstances that would insure its publicity. Please understand me Mrs. Telfer I do not wish to hurt your feelings. You also have a husband here and I believe you have heard from him and have some idea by this time, of the actual conditions that exist now, and have existed since our departure from Portland 7 months ago, but to those responsible ones of the Red Cross and Emer. Corps, I will predict and hope for them a day when they will be heartily ashamed for the part they have taken in this matter, and I have sufficient respect for and confidence in them to believe they will do just as much toward righting this matter, when the truth is known. The facts are, you have been imposed upon, and the officers from the Colonel down grossly and ungenerously misrepresented.

For the kindness intended when this money was given the regiment, I for myself thank you very much, as it was unquestionably a great benefit, and might have been considered a blessing, but circumstances that have arisen since has compelled every captain into the expression that the later curse far over topped any previous blessings.

I have no men sick at the present time. That is to say, none requiring special attention excepting Lieut. Haynes.[188] He is threatened with typhoid and will be taken to the Hospital this P.M. His wife arrived two days ago. As for the company's Mess, my company has saved on their allowances, (Or rather they have sold off the surplus which they did not need and after purchasing fruits fresh, canned and dried, milk, eggs etc.) over $100.00 which constitutes a Company Mess Fund, and as the Government allows extra rations to the sick at the rate of 30 cents per day, we have more money than we have any need of.

If you please Mrs. Telfer, no part of this letter is for publication. I have no objection to any one's reading it, that you may care to show it to.

Assuring you of my esteem and well wishes, and hoping earnestly to be able at some future day to explain satisfactorily matters too tedious in detail for the pen, I beg to sign myself, respectfully

Your Obedient Servant
W. S. Moon
Capt 2d Or USV Co C

AT CAMP NEWPORT

Pleasant Experiences & Vicissitudes of Soldiers'
Life at the Seaside [189]

Camp Newport
August 25, 1895

To the Editor of The Herald.

The hour is guard-mount, six thirty o'clock P.M.,
Mr. Remington is down on the beach. I must therefore dispense with illustrations of the stirring military
scenes from this seat of war. The camp is on an elevation 40 feet above the Bay, just south of the Ocean
House. Last evening Lieut. Phillips, on behalf of the
boys, kindly invited us up to dinner. The long mess
table fairly groaned with its burden of substantials.
The sea air had begun to sharpen our naturally good
appetite, and rock oyster soup, hash and straight
bread and butter with coffee was relished more than
an elaborate dinner could be away from this out-of-
door, seaside life. Saturday evening many of the soldiers appeared at the ball in uniform, and the boys in
blue were here, as elsewhere, much sought by the
ladies and respected by all. This we considered to be
the result of the dignified bearing of the entire command. We were too late for roll call next morning but
saw the drill. It was ended about quarter past eight,
it being Sunday morning, and then everybody was
off duty until after lunch. At that time a short drill
was given for the entertainment of the excursion
party which had arrived at noon.

In the evening the company went together to the
Presbyterian church. A large party of ladies under
the chaperonage of Mrs. J. K. Weatherford called at
the camp after the evening service and spent an hour
inspecting the camp. Afterwards all were invited
to the Colonel's tent. Miss Mary Cundiff recited a
charming little selection appropriate to the occasion.
Several members of the company contributed to a
short programme which was followed by a short
speech by the commanding officer, Colonel Geo. F.
Telfer, in the happy way of one who always knows
how to say the right thing at the right time in a fitting
manner. Refreshments were served before the guests
departed. The visitors left, the camp lights gradually
disappeared. Here and there in muffled solemn quiet,
a solitary guard walking his lonely sentinel, but made
the stillness greater. Had it been our good fortune to
have the pass word, we would have gone within the
lines, called on Lieutenant Phillips and asked him to
arouse the camp with a midnight alarm to dispel the
gloom of the hour, but we couldn't and the guard
said us nay.

Archibald Forbes, Jr.

Aug 26, 1896

The militia boys returned from the bay Monday noon where they have been for ten days on an encampment. The camp was beautifully located near the Ocean House and members of Co. F, and the hospital corps of this city, C of Eugene and B and I of Salem were present. H. J. Moore, formerly of the Corvallis Agricultural College cooked for the camp. Col. G. O. Yoran of Eugene was in command of camp. T. H. Rodes was Quartermaster Sargeant and J. A. Finch, commissary. 65 men were in line. Gov. Lord, Major Jackson, and Gen. Tuttle reviewed the companies at Ocean House Wednesday morning. The encampment perhaps was fair from a military standpoint, but socially it was a dismal failure. Last year visitors were entertained royally by the company but this year a gloom usually unknown to camp life, enshrouded the camp. Col. Geo. Telfer had command of the camp last year and knew just how to make everybody happy. While Col. Yoran is a splendid fellow perhaps, he is entirely inexperienced in military matters and failed to grasp the idea that a volunteer encampment where each individual defrayed his own expenses, should not be as strictly military in many details as though the state footed the bills. The idea of volunteer encampments first started with Co. F, when the boys camped at the fair grounds last year. Then after that encampment proved such a success the Newport camp followed in August proving to be a splendid means of education to the soldier boys. When the encampment was proposed this year, an invitation was tendered the Eugene and Salem companies to go as our guests similar to last year's method. But Col. Yoran at once set down on this project and flatly stated that he would not tolerate the idea one moment. Dissatisfaction arose at once throughout the detachment and matters grew worse constantly. Col. Yoran mistook a letter from Gen. Beebe for an order for the encampment and the difference was never discovered until three days before the boys started for Newport. Yoran failed to get the tents or mess outfit for the outside companies, and it was then that the services of Col. Telfer had to be secured for a "go between" to ask an informal manner for the tents from brigade headquarters, which were granted.

Despite precedents last year in the Newport camp, Col. Yoran placed guards on duty the entire day and night, a thing that was not thought of last year and not needed now, only in the imaginative brain of this would-be Napoleon. Imagine a camp organized for mutual education and pleasure patroled constantly, merely because this commander desired to exert his feeble authority. Even before the arrival of the main body this soldier chief aroused the ire of every militiaman in his regiment by stating "that if any of the boys insulted or otherwise acted 'fly' with the campers at the bay they would be confined to the guard house at once," showing a lack of confidence in the men who he is expected to lead and from whom he expects respect and honor. The best thing that could happen to the Second Regiment would be the resignation of Yoran and the placing of some practical man in command and until such happens nothing but disorder and confusion can exist.

He is credited with saying that he would never be a party again to such an awkward review as was witnessed on Wednesday by the officers and it is to be hoped that the next review will find another, more learned in common courtesy if nothing else, commanding the enterprising Second Regiment, one who will not bring disgrace upon himself and his men by his gross ignorance.

TO ALL WHOM IT MAY CONCERN: [190]

KNOW YE, That *George F. Telfer*, a *First Lieutenant* of *Company L.* of the *Second* Regiment of *Oregon Infantry* Volunteers, who was enrolled on the *Twenty Seventh* day of *April*, one thousand eight hundred and ninety-*Eight*, to serve *Two years*, or during the war, is hereby DISCHARGED from the service of the United States, by reason of *Muster out of Regiment*.

No objection to his reenlistment is known to exist.

The said *George F. Telfer* was born in *Buffalo*, in the State of *New York* and when enrolled was *43 2/12* years of age, *5* feet *7* inches high, *Fair* complexion, *Dark Blue* eyes, *Dark Brown* hair, and by occupation a *Salesman*.

GIVEN at *The Presidio San Francisco Cal* this *Seventh* day of *August, 1899*.

> *O. Summers*
> *Colonel*
> Commanding the *Regiment*.

Countersigned:
C. L. Beckruts
Captain 16th Infantry U.S.A.
Mustering Officer.

MILITARY RECORD

Commissioned Officer:

Distinguished service:

Battles, engagements, skirmishes, expeditions: *Served* during the Spanish American war 1898 in the Philippines Guam L. I. June 20, Manila August 13, 1898, Served during the Philippine Insurrection 1899. Manila Feby 4 and 5, Tondo Feby 22, Guadaloupe March 13, Malapat Na Bato March 14, Pasig Mar. 15, Laguna De Bahia Mar 19, Malabon Mar. 25, Palo March 26, Marilao April 11, Santa Maria April 12, Morzagaray Apr. 23 24 and 25 Maronco April 27 San Rafael May 1, Baliuag May 2, Maasim May 4, Salacat May 15, Tabon Bridge May 16, San Isidro May 17, San Antonia May 20, Arayat May 21, 1899.

Wounds received in service: *No*

Remarks: *Service Honest and Faithful*

> *O. Summers*
> *Colonel*
> Commanding *Regiment*

State of Washington }
County of Kitsap   } SS

This is to certify that the above is a true and correct copy of the army discharge of George F. Telfer.

(signature here)
_____
Notary Public in and for the State of Washington, residing at Retsil

Notes

1. *See* Appendix for examples.

2. Morning *Oregonian*, 29 April 1898, p. 5, col. 1. Hereafter, *Oregonian*, 5/1.

3. *Oregonian*, 7 May 1898, 8/1.

4. *Annual Report of Major General E. S. Otis, USV, Dept. of the Pacific & Eighth Army Corps* . . . Manila, P.I. 1899, 4.

5. *Oregonian*, 13 November 1898, 8/2.

6. *Oregonian*, 13 November 1898, 8/2.

7. *Oregonian*, 11 January 1899, 10/1.

8. *Oregonian*, 27 April 1898, 7/3.

9. *Oregonian*, 13 November 1898, 8/1.

10. Milwaukie *Sentinel*, 26 March 1899.

11. Milwaukie *Sentinel*, 26 March 1899.

12. The measles began at Camp McKinley in Portland. Between Guam and the Philippines the 49th and last case was reported. *Oregonian*, Portland, 24 Aug. 1898, 8/1.

13. Probably William W. Darling, manager, Overman Wheel Co., who resided at 805 2nd. in Portland. (*Polk's Portland City Directory*, 1898.)

14. Major-General Henry Clay Merriam, USA, commander, Depts. of Columbia and California responsible for forwarding troops to the Philippines, 1898. (*Who was Who in America 1897–1942*, Chicago, 1942.)

15. Wife of J. S. Raleigh, accountant, who resided at 1506 Taylor St. in San Francisco. (*Polk's San Francisco City Directory*, 1898.)

16. Mrs. Martin Winch, Sr. Mr. Winch was manager of the Simeon G. Reed Estate, and resided at 241 7th. Joseph Buchtel, was a Portland photographer and resided at 16 E 6th. (*Polk's Portland City Directory*, 1898.)

17. Second Lt. G. W. Povey of Co. L, 2nd Oregon U. S. Volunteer Infantry. Hereafter, 2nd OR USVI.

18. First Lt. and Quartermaster L. H. Knapp, 2nd OR UVSI Staff.

19. This came to pass with the capture of Guam on 20 June 1898. It was 22 June when American troops landed in Cuba.

20. U. S. Cruiser *Charleston*, Capt. Henry Glass.

21. Captain Harry L. Wells and 2nd Lt. G. W. Povey of Company L, 2nd OR USVI.

22. Mrs. Charles Reeve, wife of the colonel of the 13th Minnesota Regiment.

23. James J. Hill (1838–1916), Great Northern Railroad President (St. Paul & Pacific R. R., etc.)

24. Letter from Margaret T. Raleigh to Mrs. Geo. F. Telfer which is a fine example of the sentiments of the time is reproduced in the Appendix.

25. Duck is a linen or cotton fabric similar to canvas in appearance but lighter weight.

26. Brigadier-General Thomas M. Anderson, USV, in command of the Military in the Philippines until General Merritt arrived on 25 July 1898.

27. Lottie R. Telfer received $75 each month beginning 1 July 1898, and ending with a check dated 1 Mar. 1899, from Crocker-Woolworth National Bank in San Francisco. With the March payment went a memo dated 17 Feb. 1899, which read: "Referring to our Circular of November 16th, 1898, addressed to the Officers of the various Regiments at Manila, we think that under the present circumstances, the payments which have been made by us for the account of the Officers of the Regiments at Manila, should not be continued indefinitely. This has never been looked upon by us as a business proposition, and we cannot see our way clear to put it on that basis now. It was taken up as a temporary matter and was supposed to tide over a few months at the outside. The matter of charging the Officers for this accommodation, would not be considered for a moment; and while we are glad to have been of service in the past, we trust that you will view the matter in the proper light. Payments will be made for your account for the months of February and March, after which time please arrange to remit direct to your relatives. . . ."

28. Henry Harris Newhall was a pioneer banker who founded the Bank of East Portland. (Oregon Historical Society, Biography Folder #56, obituary of his daughter, Dorothy N. Pooley.)

29. Telfer headed his letter with this brief chronology. Note that the 28 May-1 June entries are not done in letter form, but as a shipboard diary.

30. Troops on these ships were: *City of Peking*, 1st CA USVI under Col. James F. Smith, and seventy-five sailors commanded by Lt. Holcombe, who were joining Dewey; *Australia*, Brig. Gen. Thomas M. Anderson with his staff, and two battalions of the 2nd OR USVI under Col. Owen Summers; *City of Sydney*, one battalion of the 2nd OR USVI under Maj. P. G. Eastwick, a battalion of the 15th U. S. Infantry under Captain Murphy and a detachment from Battery A Heavy Artillery under Capt. Dennis Geary. (*The Call*, San Francisco, 26 May 1898, 1/1–6.)

31. A striker was an enlisted man assigned as an officer's servant.

32. Major P. G. Eastwick, 2nd OR USVI.

33. Grace was his eldest daughter, age sixteen.

34. The Chaplain was W. S. Gilbert from Eugene.

35. Private Herbert W. Kerrigan, Co. H, 2nd OR USVI. Son of Philip J., grocer at 349 Stark. (*Polk's Portland City Directory*, 1898). He was a member of the Multnomah Amateur Athletic Club's track and field team which was Northwest Champion in 1895. Kerrigan held the record for the high jump at 6'2". (Louise Godfrey, *History of the Multnomah Amateur Athletic Club*, 1967, 9.)

36. Willis was his son, born 22 December 1884.

37. Arthur W. Pearson who in 1895 was Trade Manager for Mitchell, Lewis & Staver on Pine and 2nd in Portland. The firm sold agricultural implements, machinery and vehicles. (*Polk's Portland City Directory*, 1895). The Oregonians in Honolulu had established headquarters for the Oregon soldiers at the store of A. W. Pearson. Mr. Pearson ran a cyclery and provided free use of bicycles to the troops. (*Oregonian*, 29 June 1898, 8).

38. Otto A. Bierbach in 1891 was a clerk in Woodard, Clarke & Co., wholesale and retail druggists, 141 1st, Portland. (*Polk's Portland City Directory*, 1891).

39. Oscar King Davis in his book, *Conquest in the Pacific*, 32–33, writes:

Yesterday when we pulled out of Honolulu, the Oregon officers were a picturesque lot, they came aboard after their brief stay . . . in white duck, cotton and linen . . . in all shades of brown and speckled linen and wool crash, in seven different kinds of caps, some all white and some white and black, and scarcely any two shaped alike. They wore white canvas shoes of sharp toes, round toes and square toes, high cut and low cut; brown canvas shoes of as many varieties or more. . . . They showed also a childlike and confiding trust in the knowledge of the Chinese tailors of Honolulu as to what the 'regulation braid' is. . . . Some had brass buttons with anchors on them, others had brass buttons with guns, and some just plain brass. Some had pearl buttons and some bone. . . . All were worn with perfect unconcern and self-complacency as 'uniform'.

General Anderson took one glance around and held a short conversation with his Adjutant. At luncheon all the Oregon officers appeared in the regulation blue. It was hot, but it was uniform. This afternoon it got so hot that the General relented. Perhaps he found the blue a bit uncomfortable.

40. The Ladrones, or Marianas, are a group of fifteen islands in the Pacific. Guam and Saipan are possibly the best known to most Americans.

41. This mimics an episode in chapter 32 of *Innocents Abroad*. In *Mark Twain's Notebook* (New York, 1935), written by Samuel L. Clemens, Clemens tells of a diary he began as a boy: "Monday — Got up, washed, went to bed. Tuesday — Got up, washed, went to bed." And so he continued for an entire week. He was discouraged, he says, since "startling events appeared to be too rare, in my career, to render a diary necessary. I still reflect with pride that even at an early age I washed when I got up."

42. Wigwag — to signal by moving flags or portable lights in a coded pattern.

43. Sanford B. Dole.

44. *Exocetus volitans* can rise as high as thirty-five feet in the air. Momentum is provided by the tail, but large pectoral fins which are spread out to help maintain balance and assist in gliding, create the flying fish impression. There are some sixty-five species of "flying fish."

45. Today's navy has no such custom. Josephus Daniels, Secretary of the navy in 1913, banned all alcohol from naval vessels, and that is still the rule.

46. Major H. W. Cardwell, chief surgeon, 2nd OR USVI.

47. Commander W. C. Gibson on the *Peking* and Lt. Comm. Thomas H. Phelps, Jr. on the *City of Sydney*.

48. Private Elias Hutchinson of Co. M, 2nd OR USVI.

49. Thomas W. Johnston (Will), of Co. E, 2nd OR USVI, from Portland (*Oregonian*, 24 Aug. 1898, 8/2) was the patient. Dr. Matthew H. Ellis, major and surgeon, 2nd OR USVI performed the surgery for blocked intestines and Capt. R. E. Davis of Co. E, 2nd OR USVI, assisted.

50. Oscar King Davis, special correspondent of the *New York Sun* and *Harper's Weekly* traveled to the Philippine Islands on the *Australia* with the Oregon troops. He was given a private stateroom, entertained by the Oregon officers, "and treated as gentlemen would treat other gentlemen at all times" according to Col. Owen Summers in the lead story on p. 8 of the *Oregonian*, 5 Nov. 1898. But he fell out of favor when his dispatch published in the *New York Sun* of Aug. 17th was picked up by the *Oregonian* on 25 Aug. 1898, 8/6. It was a sensational story, very critical of volunteers in general and Oregon's volunteers in particular. He charged them with lack of discipline, looting, and disobeying orders. He asserted that rather than officers who know something of military matters and methods, "there is probably the finest lot of county politicians in the Second Oregon which has ever been gathered together in that state, or perhaps any other." His story drew rebuttal from Col. Summers, USV, Maj.-Gen. Wesley Merritt, USA, and Maj.-Gen. Thomas M. Anderson, USV. Perhaps the reason why Davis' story was written in that vein is to be found in this paragraph in Col. Summers' letter to the *Oregonian* on the above date — "I will state that after the capture of Manila he [Davis] went into a Spaniard's house in the city, represented himself to be a lieutenant-colonel of the U. S. Army, and undertook to take possession and drive out the family, and it became my duty as provost marshal to put him out of the house."

51. It was actually eleven Spanish naval vessels sunk, with three hundred men killed and four hundred wounded. Six Americans were wounded, none killed. The Spanish fleet battle line was in front of Cavite, so as not to endanger Manila. The Spanish had removed all navigational lights at the harbor entrance in the expectation that this would deter Dewey from sailing in at night, for fear of running aground. Deeming this adequate protection, the forts at the harbor entrance were only lightly manned. So, Dewey's squadron sailed safely into the bay during the night, with only token firing from the fort at El Fraile rock and Punta Restinga commanding the Boca Raton entrance which his squadron used. At daylight on 1 May 1898, the Americans engaged the Spanish ships and batteries at Cavite, and by noon Dewey's ships were anchored off Manila.

52. In August 1896, several Filipino groups united in revolt against the monopoly which Spanish friars held over agricultural land in the islands. Initially there was no intent to become independent of Spain, but to restrict the power of the church, and gain more say in their own governance for the

Filipinos. The tactics of guerrilla warfare were successful initially, but the Filipinos were not equipped for a lengthy campaign. Spain negotiated a settlement in which some forty of the rebel leaders agreed to leave the islands upon payment of 400,000 pesos with another 400,000 to be paid later, and the promise that certain land and government reforms would be made. These promises were not kept, however, and in February 1898, guerrilla warfare again broke out in central Luzon.

53. Emilio Aguinaldo, born in Cavite March 1869, graduate of College of San Juan. President of provisional government, 1897. Invited by Dewey to join him against Spain. On 11 May 1898 Aguinaldo landed at Cavite and took command of the insurgent army.

54. First Lt. August B. Gritzmacher and 2nd Lt. J. A. McKinnon.

55. Probably siblings of the two lieutenants are among the school friends of his daughter, Grace.

56. Irving H., Douglas L., and Martin Pratt.

57. A military order, number 23, dated 10 April 1885. On the back side, this letter to Willis was written.

58. The steamer *China* brought the Pennsylvania and Colorado troops.

59. Captains Harry L. Wells, Herbert L. Heath and Austin Prescott.

60. Nut-like seed of the betel palm.

61. Soldiers were instructed not to sleep on the ground because of the malarial mosquito problem. Mosquito netted cots were a preventive measure. For this and other health hazards, *see* Dr. Cardwell's letter to Brigadier-General Beebe published in the *Oregonian*, 11 January 1899.

62. The famous Portland Hotel, between 6th and Broadway, Morrison and Yamhill.

63. These poisonous fish were probably *physalia*, or Portugese Man of War which will paralyze prey with stinging capsules shot out from polyps.

64. Major-General Wesley Merritt was senior ranking officer in the Army in 1898. Shortly after the occupation of Manila Merritt departed for Paris and the Peace Conference, turning over command in the Philippines to Maj.-Gen. Otis.

65. Camphor-ice is an ointment of camphor, castor oil, and other ingredients, to relieve itching.

66. F. W. Vaille established the first American Post Office in the Philippine Islands. He was a former Portlander. A letter recounting his experiences appeared in the *Oregonian* of 11 Sept. 1898, 24/3.

67. Lighters are flat bottom boats or barges used to unload vessels not lying at wharves.

68. Household troops were those appointed to attend and guard a sovereign or his residence.

69. Captain G. F. Case, Co. F, 2nd OR USVI

70. Colonel Owen N. Summers, brevet brig.-gen. USV.

71. Colonel Charles McC. Reeve, 13th Minnesota USVI, from Minneapolis.

72. Two factors caused this. First, they wanted a chance to fight. Peace with Spain had been concluded, but it was obvious that there would be battles with the native insurgents. Second, they realized that the Philippine Islands could become the new frontier for commercial opportunity, and they would have first-hand experience of the country and culture to offer any employer or investor.

73. R. J. Fitzgerald, major and surgeon, 13th Minnesota USVI, from Minneapolis. While on board the transport *City of Para* he was assigned as Chief Operating Surgeon of the 8th Army Corps, to serve at Camp Dewey. (Karl Irving Faust, *Campaigning in the Phillipines*, San Francisco, 1899, 52.) Henry C. Cabell, 3rd USAI, was with Brigadier-General Wheaton's Brigade.

74. Klondike or Yukon was a small sheet iron stove with an oven in the pipe, which was carried by prospectors in the Yukon.

75. The Luneta is a park and promenade on the shore of the bay just outside the walled city.

76. Trifles or oddments; frivolous food in the meat and potato cuisine of that period.

77. The *Oregonian*, 22 July 1898 reports that Heath, Prescott, Wells and Telfer overstayed their leave by two days and were confined to quarters, facing probability of court-martial. (Oregon Historical Society pamphlet file, Spanish-American War Folder). *See* 18 July 1898 letter for Telfer's account of this leave.

78. This letter, written 11 Sept., was received in Portland on 24 Sept.

79. Pierre N. Boeringer was a war artist with the Philippine Expedition and represented the *San Francisco Call* and the *New York Herald*. (*Oregonian*, 5 Nov. 1898, 8/3).

80. Mrs. Henry E. Jones, president of the Oregon Emergency Corps, which was organized 17 April 1898 by a group of "patriotic women of Portland" to assist Oregon soldiers and their families. (*Minutes of the OEC*, in the Oregon Historical Society Manuscript Collection). Mrs. George F. Telfer was among the 12 elected to the executive committee. Local auxiliaries were organized throughout the state. A year later the group affiliated with the Red Cross.

81. Lieutenant E. P. Crowne, adjutant, 2nd OR USVI.

82. *Munsey's* magazine, a general, illustrated monthly which ran a serial history of the war from October 1898 to August 1899 with many military and naval illustrations. It cost 10¢. The only monthly with greater circulation was *The Ladies Home Journal*.

83. Captain Austin F. Prescott, Co. D, 2nd OR USVI, from La Grande.

84. Lieutenant Merrill D. Phillips, Co., I, 2nd OR USVI, from Albany, and Lt. Col. George O. Yoran

85. He must mean Capt. C. E. McDonell of Co. H. There was no McDonald in the 2nd OR USVI. McDonell was a member of the Multnomah Amateur Athletic Club. The *Oregonian*, 4 Mar. 1899, 8/1, printed a letter from him thanking MAAC for money donated and reporting on sports and life in Manila.

86. Sanford Whiting, Capt. and Asst. Surgeon, 2nd OR USVI. Story about his work in the smallpox hospital appeared in *Oregonian* of 11 Mar. 1899, 8/1.

87. Lieutenant Albert J. Brazee, battalion adjutant, 2nd OR USVI and Lt. William A. Huntley, Co. I, 2nd OR USVI, from Oregon City.

88. Lieutenant E. W. Moore, Co. F, 2nd OR USVI, was sent home on sick leave. Interview in *Oregonian*, 19 Oct. 1898. He and Lt. Edgar J. Bryan of Co. E were responsible for producing complete maps of the Spanish and insurgent works and the country surrounding Manila in time for General Merritt's arrival.

89. General Charles Reeve, former colonel of 13th Minnesota USVI, appointed head of Provost Guard, Manila.

90. Captain L. L. Pickens, Co. I, 2nd OR USVI.

91. Andrew Kan & Co., established 1882, Hong Kong and Yokohama Importing House, 4th and Morrison Streets. (*Polk's Portland City Directory*, 1898)

92. Sergeant J. Edward Gantenbein, Co. H, 2nd OR USVI.

93. Lieutenant Richard H. Barber, Co. G, 2nd OR USVI. Physician, 716 Marquam Bldg., resided 1231 Cleveland Ave., Portland (*Polk's Portland City Directory*, 1898). Born in 1863, Worcester, England, M. D. Edinburgh. Practised in Gardiner, Oregon. Held Chair of Pediatrics and Hygiene at Willamette University (unattributed news clipping Oregon Historical Society Biography File).

94. The Chief Surgeon, USV, Herbert Caldwell, stated that "Trained male nurses, who can be enlisted in the corps and subjected to discipline, not Red Cross nurses, would be gratefully received and put to work." (*Oregonian*, 11 January 1899, 10/2.)

95. Fever bands were strips of flannel permeated with drops of camphor or eucalyptus oil which were worn across the chest in the belief they would prevent fevers. (We thank Mr. Stammerjohan, Office of Interpretive Services, California State Department of Parks and Recreation, for this information.)

96. Lieutenant Thomas N. Dunbar, Co. E, 2nd OR USVI.

97. This was a Telfer family prejudice. The eating of peanuts was considered improper, possibly because of the prevalence of peanuts in saloons. It was a prejudice passed along through at least three generations.

98. *See Oregonian*, 25 August 1898 for the New York *Sun* story.

99. Letters from Colonel Summers, General Merritt, and General Anderson were published in the *Oregonian*, 5 Nov. 1898, 8/1.

100. Major-General Elwell S. Otis, USV took command in Philippine Islands when Merritt left for the Paris Peace Conference.

101. Captain William S. Moon, Co. C, 2nd OR USVI. His letter appeared in the *Oregonian*, 16 Nov. 1898, 8/1.

102. Lieutenant Colonel James Jackson, 2nd Cavalry

USA served as instructor of Oregon National Guard for five years, retired 21 Sept. 1897. Succeeded by Lt. H. C. Cabell, 14th Infantry, late of Vancouver Barracks. (Oregon Historical Society Scrapbook 9, p. 5).

103. Lieutenant Fielding S. Kelly, Battalion Adjutant, 2nd Or USVI.

104. A.B. Gritzmacher, 1st Lt., Co. H., 2nd Oregon USVI.

105. Appeared in *Oregonian*, 5 Nov. 1898, 8/1.

106. Stomach bands were flannel, worn around the belly and thought to ward off disease. In 1902 the Army decided that the belly bands would be more successful if they were orange colored. However, the dye ran as the men perspired, so eventually that variation was abandoned. (Source as in 95.)

107. Lt. Lawrence H. Knapp, Quarter Master, 2nd OR USVI.

108. A "pug" is a close knot or coil of hair.

109. Mrs. Agnes Swinton, widow of Robert C., lived at 1259 Williams Ave. (*Polk's Portland City Directory*, 1898). Mrs. Barber was the wife of Lt. Richard H. Barber of Co. G, 2nd OR USVI.

110. John Beeson was a great-uncle of Lottie Telfer. He lived in Wisconsin.

111. Story about the arrival of Mrs. Knapp and Mrs. Haines appeared in the *Oregonian*, 17 Jan. 1899, 9/5.

112. Captain William Gadsby, Col. G, 2nd OR USVI.

113. High Binders were members of a band of Chinese criminals or terrorists principally in California. Immigrant Chinese laborers who could not fulfill their debt contracts were subjected to violence by High Binders.

114. This opinion also espoused in *The Spanish-American War: A Compact History*. *See* Bibliography.

115. Secretary of War, Russell A. Alger was severely criticized by the public and press for inefficiency and mismanagement of supplying and transporting troops in this first war overseas. He finally resigned 19 July 1899. He was secretary of war from 5 Mar. 1897 until 1 Aug. 1899.

116. Willis (the editor's father) became a naval architect. He was general manager of ship-building and naval architect at Commercial Iron Works during World War II.

117. Enfalading: to rake with gunfire in the direction the length of a line of troops.

118. Quick lime is a caustic, highly infusible form of calcium carbonate. It develops great heat when wet.

119. Strychnine was used as a tonic to stimulate the central nervous system.

120. *Oregonian*, 22 Sept. 1898, 4/2.

121. *See* note 50.

122. St. David's Episcopal Church, on Morrison between E. 12 and E. 13th. Rev. George B. Van Waters, rector, (*Polk's Portland City Directory*, 1898).

123. *Oregonian*, 15 Oct. 1898, 8/2.

124. *Oregonian*, 15 Oct. 1898, 8/2.

125. Private Alex B. Galloway, Co. L, 2nd OR USVI.

126. Joseph Simon (1851–1935), U.S. Senator 1898–1903, mayor of Portland, 1909–1911, state senator 1880–98, and president of senate for five sessions.

127. Brigadier General Charles F. Beebe, Oregon National Guard, president, the Chas. F. Beebe Co., Shipping & Commercial Ship Chandlers, Insurance Agents, and Co's Dispatch Line of Clipper Ships from New York and Philadelphia, 1st N. W. cor. Ankeny. (*Polk's Portland City Directory*, 1898).

128. *See* note 85.

129. Quinine head was caused by incorrect dosage. The men's eyes would turn yellowish and their skin turn slightly jaundiced. Source same as 95.

130. Major Julian M. Cabell, brigade surgeon, USV, assistant surgeon, 1st Reserve Hospital, Manila.

131. Dr. Frances E. Woods, Portland nurse sent to Manila by the OEC. Miss Lana Killian, nurse sent to Manila by the OEC, with Dr. Woods.

132. *See Oregonian*, 11 Oct. 1898, 5/5.

133. Mrs. Jones's letter is not available, but one can surmise its contents were based upon rumors propagated by enlisted men's letters home. Parents sometimes forwarded these letters to the *Oregonian* or wrote to the newspaper expressing indignation over the reported condition of the Oregon Volunteers in Manila. The gist of the rumors was that officers lived high on the hog while the men went hungry, and that the offi-

cers appropriated for their own riotous living the $1200 which the OEC. (Mrs. Jones, president) had given the regiment. Each Captain had been given $100 from this fund to be used for his company's welfare. He was instructed to report on its use to a designated officer of the OEC.

134. *See* Capt. Moon's letter (Appendix) responding to a letter from Mrs. Telfer of 1 November.

135. There were several letters in the *Oregonian* of 25 Oct. 1898, on page 8, which could have started this exchange. Notably, one by a parent, G. G. Ferguson, relating conditions of troop transport to Manila, and saying — "a man in command of troops . . . should forgo occasionally champagne and ice cream, to see how the boys are faring". He claimed the boys had only two hardtack and a potato and coffee twice a day. Another letter from a "Co. I Webfooter" claimed some officers must be profitting from starving the soldiers.

136. Lieutenant Ralph Platt, commissary for the Oregon regiment aboard the "Australia".

137. "Portland Nurse at Manila cables for Aid" was headline in *Oregonian*, 18 Oct. 1898, 12/1. Dr. Frances E. Woods cabled to the president of the OEC.

138. *See* Appendix, letter from Moon.

139. This letter of 7 December was written before he had seen the OEC Press Committee statement in the *Oregonian* of 16 November 1898, 8/1.

140. The OEC sent $600.00 to Manila with Mrs. Knapp. (*OEC Minutes*, 10/29/98, Bk. II, 29).

141. Lieutenant Fred W. Sladen, Aide-de-Camp to Major Gen. Otis, Mustering Officer. Joseph A. Sladen was clerk of U. S. Circuit Court and resided at 722 Flanders in Portland. (*Polk's Portland City Directory*, 1898).

142. Colonel Jackson was the newly appointed inspector-general on the staff of the Commander-in-Chief of the Oregon National Guard (Governor). He had "a vast knowledge of military details, particularly in respect to the Guard of this state" according to the *Oregonian*, 27 April 1898.

143. Captain John M. Poorman, Co. M, 2nd OR USVI.

144. Eliot W. Ordway, Co. H, 2nd OR USVI, of Portland, was invalided out. He died at sea of typhoid while en route home. (*Oregonian*, 14 Feb. 1899, 16/1.) Portrait sketch and biography in *Oregonian*, 23 Oct. 1898, 1/3.

145. Charles B. Franklin, corporal, Co. L, 2nd OR USVI.

146. On 14 Nov. 1898, Lottie read to the OEC a letter from her Captain Moon of Co. C., explaining his actions regarding the $100.00 and enclosing a full statement of his stewardship. The OEC found it satisfactory. (OEC Minutes, Bk. II, 49).

147. Captain William D. McKinnon, chaplain, 1st Regiment, CA USVI.

148. Major Percy G. Willis, 2nd OR USVI.

149. Trinity Episcopal Church, N. E. corner 6th and Oak, The Rev. D. Claiborne Garrett, Rector. (*Polk's Portland City Directory*, 1898).

150. Mrs. James Hackney asked Mrs. McKinley to use her influence to get her son, Sloan Hackney, discharged. She had heard he was sick, or dead, and had no way of finding out. Claimed he had been without food four days and had to stand in trenches with mud and water up to his waist for twenty-four hours so no wonder he was sick. . . . (*Oregonian*, 18 Nov. 1898, 8/2.)

151. *See Oregonian*, 8 Jan. 1899, 24/1, for brief biography of Lee Keeney Morse.

152. *See* note 27.

153. Mary C. Flavel, widow of Capt. George Flavel, and her daughters, Nellie and Kate. They resided at 215 8th in Astoria. Today's Flavel House museum.

154. L. K. G. Smith, fomerly president of Resenfeld-Smith Co., Wholesale Tobacco and Cigars, 41 Front St., Portland.

155. C. F. DeMay, acting asst. surgeon, USA.

156. Anthony Thompson Glaze of Fond du Lac, Wisconsin, founding editor of the *Ripon Commonwealth*.

157. Captain William Gadsby, Co. G, 2nd OR USVI, resigned command of his company on surgeon's orders, and returned home. In an interview in the *Oregonian*, 29 Nov. 1898, 12/2–3, he described the condition of Oregon volunteers in Manila.

158. Simeon E. Josephi, physician and surgeon, dean of medical department University of Oregon, resided 132 E. 12th, Portland. (*Polk's Portland City Directory*, 1898).

The captaincy eluded Telfer, but all this "influence" had some effect—the *Oregonian*, 15 Aug. 1899, 12/1, carried a story headlined "Plum for a Volunteer, Lt. George F. Telfer to be Census Supervisor, Congressman Moody and Two Oregon Senators Decide to Recommend Him for the First District." The reporter writes that: "The position is one which has been eagerly sought for and for which the number of applicants was exceedingly large. . . . Although but recently returned from Manila, Mr. Telfer's campaign has not been neglected, as his friends have been pressing his claims for some time. . . . This is the first political appointment to come to a volunteer, and the promptness with which it was made is a straw which probably shows which way the political wind is likely to blow in the future."

159. *See* "Letter written by an officer of the Second Oregon to his wife", in the *Oregonian*, 15 Oct. 1898, 8/2, 1 Dec. 1898, 8/2, and 5 Dec. 1898, 1/1.

160. A letter from Capt. Harry Wells was read to the OEC meeting of 10 Jan. 1899. (OEC Minutes, BK II, 88).

161. Hiram E. Mitchell of Mitchell, Tanner & Mitchell, lawyers. Resided at 334 E 13th. (*Polk's Portland City Directory*, 1898).

162. Delsarte refers to a system of movement patterned on the theories of Francois Delsarte (1811–71), a French teacher of dramatic and musical expression. His teachings were a precursor to what was later called modern dance.

163. On the night of 4 Feb. 1899, the Insurgents commenced action against the Americans in Manila. The first shot was fired by the natives from Block-house No. 6 at Santa Mesa where the Nebraska regiment manned the outposts. (Douglas White, *On to Manila*, San Francisco, 1899).

164. Brigadier General Robert P. Hughes was responsible for the policing of Manila during the February Insurgent battles. He had been General Merritt's Inspector General at San Francisco and was commended for his instruction of green troops. (House of Representatives, 56th Congress 1st session, Doc. #2, Serial #3902, Annual Reports of War Dept. *Report of Secretary of War, 1898*.)

165. Brigadier General Irving Hale, USV, commanding 2nd Brigade, 2nd Divison, under Maj. Gen. Arthur Mac-Arthur. The Brigade included the First South Dakota, First Colorado, 1st Nebraska regiments of volunteers, and one of Utah's Batteries. (White, *On to Manila*) (Maj. Gen. E. S. Otis, USV, *Annual Report of the Military Governor in the Philippine Islands*, Manila, 1899.)

166. *See* the two-page story about the fighting in and near Manila, dated 12 Feb., published in the *Oregonian*, 21 Mar. 1899, 8/9.

167. Brigadier General Charles King, USV. His Brigade was part of the First Division under command of General Anderson, and included: First Washington, First California, First Idaho, and Dyer's Battery of the Sixth Artillery and Hawthorne's Mountain Battery. White, *P. I. Military Governor's Report*, 1899, 69 and *On to Manila*.

168. Colonel Frederick W. Ames, 13th Minnesota USVI.

169. More commonly known as the Civil War, or the War Between the States.

170. The Biondo District. (*P.I. Military Governor's Report*, 1899, 183).

171. General Hughes. (*P.I. Military Governor's Report, 1899*).

172. Major Edwin S. Bean, 13th Minnesota USVI.

173. He probably refers to the Hull bill which called for expansion of the army.

174. Wheaton's Brigade consisted of: 20th and 22nd Regiments of Infantry, three troops of the 4th Cavalry, a section of light battery D, 6th Artillery, two battalions of the Washington and seven companies of the Oregon Volunteers. Brigadier General Lloyd Wheaton, USV was in command of this provisional brigade. (*P.I. Military Governor's Report*, 1899).

175. Grand Army of the Republic—organization of the Union veterans of the Civil War.

176. H. B. Taylor, Co. L, 2nd OR USVI

177. Krag-Jorgenson rifles. Col. William E. Birkhimer, inspector general of the Dept. of the Pacific & Eighth Army Corps reported to the adjutant General on 13 Aug. 1899: " . . . the retention of the Springfield in the hands of any of our troops is a great error. The smokeless powder cartridge is not a success in it and its range is faulty. To be forced to endure an enemy's fire and be powerless to damage him in return is placing too much upon any man, and the way in which the

volunteers have stood up against this and gone to the front in the face of it cannot be too highly praised." *P. I. Military Governor's Report*, appendix.

178. Harry R. Lewis was manager of Lewis & Dryden Printing Co. He resided at 40 E. 31st. (*Polk's Portland City Directory*, 1898).

179. Lieutenant J. C. Young, Co. A, 2nd OR USVI.

180. "The sun, field rations, physical exertion, and the abnormal excitment arising from almost constant exposure to fire action, have operated to bring about a general enervation from which men do not seem to recover." (*P. I. Military Governor's Report*, 1899, 202.)

181. "The most unsatisfactory part of the uniform has been the helmet and this is due to its shape. The back brim is not broad enough, and should be enlarged so as to fully shade the back of the head and neck. . . . " (*P.I. Military Governor's Report*, 1899, Appendix D, Quartermaster's Report, 25).

182. Major General Henry W. Lawton, USV, commanding First Division.

183. The terms of enlistment of the state volunteer units expired when the Treaty of Peace was ratified on April 11, 1899, but the situation with the Insurgents made it impossible to send them home until more regiments were sent to the islands. During May 1899, many more regular army troops arrived, so it was possible to implement the War Department promise to discharge the volunteers. Processing was begun on 25 May. Departure of the troops was to be in the order of arrival in the Philippines. This meant the Oregonians would be the first to return, sailing on 14 June from Manila, just ahead of the typhoon season. There had been a delay of several days while the 2nd Oregon decided whether to sail for San Francisco or Portland. (*P. I. Military Governor's Report*, 224–5).

184. The Telfer family moved to 66 E. 30th. They had been living with George's mother at 48 E. 9th N.

185. The *Oregonian* carried stories about the return of the 2nd Oregon for weeks. Elaborate plans were made for the expected arrival by ship at Portland, and when the decision to land at San Francisco was announced, acrimony was instantaneous! On 23 July 1899, an editorial deplored the scurrilous comments that the *Oregonian*'s abuse of the McKinley administration caused troops to be mustered out in San Francisco; or that the *Oregonian* wanted the Southern Pacific to get money for troop transport. Actually, it was the fact that the men would receive extra pay by mustering out in San Francisco which determined the matter. And, the welcome home was no less hearty — there were ceremonies at each stop the train made on the trip north through Oregon. Thursday, 10 Aug. was declared a public holiday by Governor Theodore Geer to welcome the troops — an elegant reception and banquet was put on at the Armory in Portland for the returned volunteers, with food prepared by the Portland Hotel staff.

186. Wife of J.S. Raleigh, accountant, who resided at 1506 Taylor St. in San Francisco. (*Polk's San Francisco City Directory*, 1898.)

187. Newspaper in Eugene, Oregon. Moon writes that it was the *Eugene Guard*, but the OEC Minutes of 27 Aug. 1898, Bk. I, 177 include a letter from Herbert Condon of the *Eugene Register* relating to the charges concerning Capt. Moon's disregard of the welfare of his company.

188. Fred W. Haynes, 2nd Lt., Co. C, 2nd OR USVI.

189. From the [Albany] *Weekly Herald-Disseminator*, Vol. XV, No. 44, 29 Aug. 1895.

190. From Spanish American War Records, National Archives, Washington, D.C.

Bibliography

Alger, R. A. *The Spanish-American War*. New York: Harper & Brothers Publishers, 1901.

Annual Report of Major General E. S. Otis, U.S. Volunteers, Commanding Department of the Pacific & 8th Army Corps, Military Governor in the Philippine Islands. Manila, P. I.: 1899 and 1900, Washington, D. C., Government Printing Office.

Davis, Oscar King. *Our Conquests in the Pacific*. New York: Frederick A. Stokes Company, 1899.

Elliot, Charles Burke. *The Philippines to the End of the Military Regime*. Indianapolis: Bobbs-Merrill Company, 1916.

Freidel, Frank. *The Splendid Little War*. Boston: Little, Brown & Company, 1958.

Funston, Frederick. *Memories of Two Wars — Cuban & Philippine Experiences*. New York: Scribners, 1914.

Gantenbein, C. U. *Oregon Volunteers in the Spanish War & Philippine Insurrection*. Salem: W. H. Leeds State Printer, 1902.

Keller, Alan. *The Spanish-American War: A Compact History*. New York: Hawthorn Books, Inc., 1969.

LeRoy, James A. *The Americans in the Philippines, A History Of The Conquest And First Years of Occupation With An Introductory Account Of the Spanish Rule*. New York: AMS Press, 1970.

Linderman, Gerald F. *The Mirror of War, American Society and The Spanish-American War*. Ann Arbor: University of Michigan Press, 1974.

Minutes of the Oregon Emergency Corps. Oregon Historical Society, Portland MSS937B.

Reports of the War Department, 55th Congress, 3rd Session, House Documents vol. 2 #2, Serial Catalogs #3744, and 3745.

Reports of the War Department. 56th Congress, 1st Session. Serial #3902.

Storey, Moorfield & Marcial P. Lichuaco. *The Conquest of the Philippines by the U.S., 1898–1925*. New York: G. P. Putnam & Sons, 1926.

Wells, Harry L. *The War in The Philippines*. San Francisco: Sunset, 1899.

White, Douglas. "On To Manila!" *Pacific Historical Magazine*, vol. 1, no. 1 (30 June 1899).

Index

Italicized page numbers refer to illustrations.

Colophon

The typeface used for both text and display in *Manila Envelopes* is Cochin. First issued by Ludwig and Mayer and other founders in 1922, it was also known as Sonderdruck and Moreau-le-Jeune. Cochin was named for Charles Nicholas Cochin (1715-90), the most famous member of a family of engravers who were the first to produce engraved title-pages. Cochin was best known for his engravings and vignettes in Denis Diderot's French *Encyclopedia* and for his editions of Boileau, Tasso, and Aristo. Cochin's work had great influence on the development of decorative type, and the italic Cochin reflects the influence of engraving.

The production of *Manila Envelopes* was accomplished through the cooperation and professional skill of the following:

Typesetting:	G & S Typesetters, Inc. Austin, Texas
Paper:	Unisource Portland, Oregon
Printing:	WCP Tualatin, Oregon
Binding:	Lincoln & Allen Portland, Oregon
Cartography:	John Tomlinson and Johanna Neshyba

Produced and designed by the Oregon Historical Society Press.